Quarterly Essay

1   POLITICAL ANIMAL
    The Making of Tony Abbott
    David Marr

101   CORRESPONDENCE
    John Wanna, Mark McKenna, Greg Jericho, Percy Allan,
    Michael Keating, Andrew Leigh, John Burnheim, Laura Tingle

135   Contributors

Quarterly Essay is published four times a year by Black Inc., an imprint of Schwartz Media Pty Ltd. Publisher: Morry Schwartz.

ISBN 978-1-86395-577-5 ISSN 1832-0953

Subscriptions – 1 year (4 issues): $59 within Australia incl. GST. Outside Australia $89. 2 years (8 issues): $105 within Australia incl. GST. Outside Australia $165.

Payment may be made by Mastercard or Visa, or by cheque made out to Schwartz Media. Payment includes postage and handling.

To subscribe, fill out and post the subscription card or form inside this issue, or subscribe online:

www.quarterlyessay.com
subscribe@blackincbooks.com
Phone: 61 3 9486 0288

Correspondence should be addressed to:

The Editor, Quarterly Essay
37–39 Langridge Street
Collingwood VIC 3066 Australia
Phone: 61 3 9486 0288 / Fax: 61 3 9486 0244
Email: quarterlyessay@blackincbooks.com

Editor: Chris Feik. Management: Sophy Williams, Jess Tran. Publicity: Elisabeth Young. Design: Guy Mirabella. Assistant Editor/Production Coordinator: Nikola Lusk. Typesetting: Duncan Blachford.

POLITICAL
ANIMAL | *The Making of Tony Abbott*

David Marr

> I am not asking the Australian people to take me on trust but on the
> record of a lifetime and an instinct to serve ingrained long before I
> became opposition leader: as a student president, trainee priest,
> Rhodes Scholar, surf life-saver and volunteer fire-fighter, as well as
> a member of parliament and as a minister in a government.
>   —Tony Abbott, to the Federal Council of the Liberal Party,
>   30 June 2012

PRINCE HAL

Australia doesn't want Tony Abbott. We never have. When pollsters rang
to ask who we wanted to take over from John Howard or Brendan Nelson
or Malcolm Turnbull we put Abbott way down the list, usually at the
bottom. As the years went by and the number of Liberal contenders
dwindled, we always wanted someone else: Peter Costello even after he
gave up the leadership without a fight; Malcolm Turnbull even after the
climate sceptics brought him undone; or Joe Hockey the untried hulk from

morning television. We never wanted the man the Liberals gave us in December 2009. Abbott was their pick, not ours. And the party was almost as stunned as the nation. "God almighty," one of the Liberals cried in the party room that day. "What have we done?"

The press pack was held behind ropes waiting for the result. Bob Ellis was treated as comic relief as he buttonholed us with predictions of an Abbott victory. All alone in a nearby anteroom the Reverend Peter Rose sat reading the Bible in front of a blank television screen. "There was no rancour in there," the priest told me. "That's what I was praying for." Hadn't the poor man noticed that parliament was a palace of rancour? It had been for weeks as Turnbull was torn to pieces by his party. Labor was gloating. Kevin Rudd was once more sailing along at the top of the polls. And the press had it wrong. The Liberal whip walked down the corridor, stood at the precise spot indicated on the carpet and announced Abbott's victory without a trace of pleasure.

Journalists swore, hit the phones and scattered. Out in the parliament gardens, pundits began talking to cameras. There was little evidence of jubilation in the corridors. Doors were closed. Abbott and the press faced each other in the party room about forty minutes later. It wasn't crowded. A little pack of supporters had come along to watch and cry "hear, hear" from time to time. They had the shattered look of people given what they'd wished for. By her new leader's side stood the deputy perpetual, Julie Bishop, smiling and smiling. As the voltage of her smile dimmed, you could see her will it back to life. Once or twice she turned on Abbott a look of coquettish amusement but her eyes were dazed.

"I accept at times I have stuffed up," he said. "I suppose I should apologise now for all my errors of the past and make a clean breast of them." But he didn't go into detail. Long practice makes him good at confession. It's in his blood. The most Catholic thing about this profoundly Catholic man is his faith in absolution. The slate can always be wiped clean. Over the years he has said and done appalling things that might have sunk another politician. But charm and candour and promises to do better have seen him forgiven so much. The loudmouth bigot of his university days, the homophobe, the blinkered Vatican warrior, the rugger-bugger, the white Australian and the junkyard dog of parliament are all, he would have us believe, consigned to the past. Another self has walked out of the wings. "The Australian public are very fair and are always prepared to give a leader of a major political party a fair go," he told his little audience. "I believe that when you become leader, you make a fresh start."

We have not seen a contender like this before. Though he admires them and studies what they teach, Tony Abbott is not another Bob Menzies or John Howard. He is more conservative than both, more quixotic and far less content with the state of the world. Heroes play a large part in his imagination. He dates the first stirrings of his interest in public life to the Ladybird books his mother read him as a child. "These usually turned out to be about great figures in history: Julius Caesar, Francis Drake and Henry V," he wrote in his book *Battlelines*. Ladybird books had been spoon-feeding heroism to children of the Empire since World War I and were still going strong in Sydney in the 1960s. "The lesson, invariably, was that duty and honour carried the day." Those ideas still excite Abbott. A few days after becoming leader of the Opposition, he was given a quick quiz by Josh Gordon of the *Sunday Age*. Favourite film? "*Gallipoli*. Seen it many times." Film star? "John Wayne." Book? "I'd have to say it's probably *Lord of the Rings*. It's the book I've read most." The best personal advice? "Avoid the occasion of sin."

Many who have loved this man for years talk of him as a romantic, a figure on a quest. Peter Costello, perhaps not so affectionately, called him "a Don Quixote ready to take on lost causes and fight for great princi-ples." Knights on horseback make odd figures in politics. They can be comic. They can be malevolent. They can be inspiring. They tend to be lonely and see their loneliness as a mark of courage. What drives them is always a little opaque: is it really much more than proving themselves to themselves? They have a way of seeing the everyday world not quite as the rest of us do. It's unsettling. Sometimes they are right and we are in their debt. Often they find themselves, lance in hand, searching for windmills. A few of these types are always about in politics, attractive bit players on the left and right. What's peculiar now is that one of them is leading the Opposition.

We didn't warm to him. Meagre satisfaction with his leadership lasted only three months as he set about his job: wrecking Labor. He saw off one of the most popular prime ministers in the history of the federation and weeks later nearly beat the man's successor at the ballot box. That 2010 campaign dashed his opponents' hopes. He didn't stuff up. He held his nerve. And he very nearly got there. In those weeks, Australians extended a measure of respect, even admiration, to him. But once that near-miss was past, the polls have been tracking our deepening dissatisfaction with the man and the job he is doing. We thought him narrow-minded and arrogant to begin with. We still do. We didn't trust him much back then and we trust him less now. Our confidence in his intelligence has sagged. All we really admire about the man is his capacity for hard work. The second week of August saw Newspoll award him a satisfaction rating of minus 24 per cent. By huge margins the people of Australia still want Turnbull and Rudd leading their parties. To be so disliked should, by all the old rules, make Abbott roadkill. He is not. Between him and the election of 2013 lies a political eternity, but as things stand now this unlikely man is heading for a magnificent victory.

What he's about is destroying a government. Looking like a prime minister in waiting is a second-order consideration. The work isn't pretty but, with a helping hand from his opponents, he has brought a million or so Australians over to his side of politics. They don't much like him but they like the Labor government even less. If Abbott can hold on all the way to the ballot box, he will be remembered as the most successful Opposition leader of the last forty years, turning a rabble into a government in four years. Tricky to read at the best of times, he's becoming more opaque as he approaches office. The big question of Australian politics now is not the fate of the mining boom or the impact of the carbon tax, but how Tony Abbott might perform as prime minister. He is campaigning hard and giving little away. Look to my record, he says, as he slogs on with a ferocity that alarms the public almost as much as it rattles the government. That's how he's chosen to play the game. Love and respect can wait.

He was Abbo to his friends. From the moment he arrived at Sydney University in the late 1970s he showed himself to be a muscular reactionary of extraordinary, boisterous energy. The study of economics and law never engaged his imagination. Politics did from the start. "He was wild," says a student from those years. "Wild even for a wild college boy." Young Tony did things hard: drinking, writing, arguing, fucking and playing rugby. His home base was St John's, the Catholic men's college under its gothic tower. His political base was the tiny Democratic Club, one of a network on campuses across the country set up and guided by Bob Santamaria's National Civic Council. For the next five years he would speak, write and campaign for NCC causes. Within days of his arrival he was putting out the club's newsletter, the *Democrat*. The background noise of the university in the years ahead was the clatter of roneo machines. The targets he chose for his March 1976 debut as a fighting journalist were lesbians, homosexuals and the Students' Representative Council (the SRC):

> Most students will be interested to know that Orientation Week's Gay dance was a financial failure. Not only did the SRC make good this loss but it collectively howled down a speaker against the motion … it is a foregone conclusion that only motions supporting subversion, perversion and revolution will be passed.

The high hopes the Abbotts had for their son had not quite been realised at Riverview, the Jesuit school in an Italian palace on the upper reaches of Sydney Harbour. Dick Abbott was a popular dentist who had taken to Catholicism in his teens. The circumstances of his conversion were peculiar. Dick's father had made a bargain with God that were his family to survive a voyage to Australia in the early months of World War II they would go over to Rome. Untouched by torpedoes, the Abbotts converted with some fervour. Dick was keen to be a priest but opted in the end for dentistry. He returned to England after the war where he met Fay "Pete"

Peters, an intelligent, energetic Australian dietician. She converted. They married. Tony was born in London in 1957. A couple of years later his mother drove the return to Australia. As Dick Abbott's practice prospered, the family moved higher up the North Shore until they were living in a beautiful house on the edge of the bush in Killara.

Three daughters were born but the family's ambitions centred on little Tony: "His mother and I knew pretty early on that, with Tony, we had produced something out of the box." The girls adored their brother. The boy worshipped his father. The mother worshipped the boy. He was in his mid-teens when his mother told a table of dentists in Sydney that Tony would one day be Pope or prime minister. There was some tension in the family between these ambitions. The girls favoured politics. Justin Rickard, a law student who dated one of the daughters at university, remembers: "Even in those days Tony was spoken very highly of in his family, with great awe and respect, and the phrase 'future PM' was often whispered or should I say yelled around the family table."

At any other school his record would have been regarded as outstanding. But at Riverview it was merely solid. He was neither head boy nor dux. Despite his father's protests, he never made the first XV or the first eight. He didn't debate. His name was not on the honour boards nor was it everywhere in the school magazine. In his final year he won the Paul Meagher Prize for Modern History and His Eminence the Cardinal's Prize for Religious Knowledge. It was not a shower of glory. The boy made his name at Riverview with a wonderful larrikin moment at speech day in October 1975. The governor-general, John Kerr, was giving the prizes in the midst of the supply crisis. "Sir John, this must be frightfully boring for you," said young Abbott as he shook the vice-regal hand. "Why don't I take you to the Liberal Party rally in town?" Kerr laughed but the quip caused quite a stir. The boy was with his mother at Reuben F. Scarf's a couple of weeks later buying a new suit for the end-of-year formal when a shop assistant broke the news that Whitlam had been sacked. "Pete" Abbott said: "Fantastic!" Tony Abbott backs Kerr to this day.

A priest at Riverview had cast his spell on the boy when he was only sixteen, a spell that has never been broken. Emmet Costello offered him an example of a priest in society, a man of faith in the world of power. Getting about Sydney in a Bentley or BMW, this heir to a gold-mining fortune from Fiji ministered to the rich, pursuing death-bed conversions in harbour mansions and bringing distinguished lapsed Catholics back into the fold. Costello's much-touted triumph was the return to mass of Tom Hughes QC, attorney-general in John Gorton's government. Costello encouraged robust faith rather than pious introspection. Habits of worship were vital. Costello's rule was: mass early and often. Life was to be lived and forgiveness was always available to the penitent. Human rights have never been Costello's bag. He's devoted to the papacy. His life's mission has been to find and shape leaders in the interests of his order and his faith.

Costello has never been shy of touting his role in the career of Tony Abbott. "I first met him in 1974 and he was then in Year 11 at Riverview and from the moment I met him he was different. He walked into my room – I was a chaplain for the boys – and he projected an image immediately of high intelligence, ambition, drive and leadership and I thought this guy is worth following." The boy was dazzled, too: here was a worldly priest confirming his own high faith in himself. One day Costello casually suggested Abbott might become a priest. The idea nagged at him for the next dozen years. Abbott would come to rate Father Costello second only to his own father as "the most important male influence on my life."

In their last weeks at school, Catholic boys of particular promise were taken aside and invited to rather mysterious "Peace with Freedom" weekends to prepare them for life at university. Though not invited, young Abbott tagged along: "Some instinct whispered that this was not an opportunity to be missed." In those summer days in early 1976 the course of his political life was set. In the heady atmosphere of that secret forum young Tony was recruited for Bob Santamaria's Movement. The men who did the work were Peter Samuel, the Bulletin's cranky political correspondent; Warren Hogan, the embattled professor of economics at Sydney University; and Joe de Bruyn, a hard-line Catholic union official about to assume lifetime leadership of the shop assistants' union. Looking back on this moment over thirty years later, Abbott wrote:

> It was a thrill to meet people of influence and authority in public life. It was exciting to think that I might be able to make a difference to the wider world. Most of all, it was good to learn that there was a way to get involved immediately through joining the Sydney University Democratic Club.

He pledged his troth to Santamaria. It would be a year before he met the man face to face but he fell in love that weekend. "I have been under the Santamaria spell ever since." He regarded him until his death in 1998 as "the greatest living Australian."

Few shared his awe. Inside and outside politics, inside and outside the Catholic Church, Santamaria was also widely hated. His venom was phenomenal; his energy inextinguishable; and his fears legion. In the Whitlam crisis just passed he had privately discussed the need to raise a secret army to defend democracy against the scourge of Labor. Now, in his sixties, he was seized by a profound sense of failure. Despite all he had done – purging communists from the unions, splitting the ALP and founding the Democratic Labor Party – he had failed in his larger purpose of ending the threat of world revolution and making Australia the good country of his Catholic dreams. His sense of mission was sustained by an absolute conviction that he stood for fundamental truth in a world of superficial values. Others might think him a fanatic, an alarmist and a bully, but his latest recruit would find him: "A philosophical star by which you could always steer."

Abbott is a man with mentors. Most were old men with embattled beliefs: true believers; relics of lost causes; men with a high view of their life and mission; men who believed in the magic of the crown, the church and old institutions. The chance to ride out with them to confront the zeitgeist touched something deep in young Tony. He was a kid with a powerful wish to serve. To stand for old ideas and old authority in the late 1970s took courage of a kind, and deep faith in faith. He believed the path Santamaria was inviting him to take was essentially religious. In the old man's obituary a couple of decades later he wrote:

> His real role was to create a type of secular religious order, something like a band of political Jesuits, a group of men and women whose religious values translated into strong commitment, not necessarily to any political party, but to a set of social principles.

The tactics were not so lofty. The Democratic Clubs were small and their membership carefully controlled. The correct line was strictly enforced. They used tactics Santamaria developed to fight Reds in the unions: provocative campaigning, ceaseless leafleting and infiltrating rival organisations. They called themselves moderates but their position was extreme: as far to the right as the Maoists and Trotskyists on campus were to the left. They were accused of rough-house tactics and wrecking what they couldn't control. The student newspaper *Honi Soit* reported: "This organisation has a long history of politically motivated violence – whether as vigilantes for vice-regals, smoke-bombers for Saigon, poster pullers for political reaction, or bullies for by-elections."

Among the young cocks on the campus, Abbott quickly made his name. Thousands of words of campaigning journalism poured out of him, an extraordinary number of them attacking homosexuals, male and female. He proudly announced the Democratic Club had established a Heterosexual Solidarity Society. When this freshman decided, with astonishing cheek, to seek election as a student fellow of the university senate, he ended his lofty manifesto by claiming: "As an infrequently practising heterosexual and drunkard I feel I have significant community of interest with many students ..." He lost the vote narrowly and his temper publicly. "He came down to the SRC and kicked a glass panel on the front door in," reported *Honi Soit*. "Not that he meant to mind you, things just seem to happen to Tony."

His fellow warriors loved him in a slightly protective way. "Tony was a warm, sociable individual, a ton of fun," recalls Joe Bullock, who is now state secretary in Western Australia of de Bruyn's shoppies' union. "People warmed to Tony. He was very personable, very quick with the common touch he still has. But he was enthusiastically hated by those who hated him. He was seen as a very worthy opponent with a capacity to win. We all thought Tony would be a force to be reckoned with when he grew up and we're still waiting." Great things seemed to be at stake. Bullock says: "Everyone thought they were engaged in a bigger battle. I thought I was engaged in a battle between good and evil."

In that late winter election season on the campus, Abbott did win a place on the SRC and in the delegation that would go in late summer to the annual conference of the Australian Union of Students (AUS). Over the next three years he would throw all his political energy into gutting both.

This mighty wrecking operation was being conducted by Democratic Clubs across Australia to prevent student representative councils channelling money to causes Santamaria feared might tear society to pieces. "It was as necessary to break the revolutionary base in the universities," he declared, "as it was to contain it in the unions." Communism still flourished in the universities and communism in all its forms – soft, hard, Russian, Maoist and Trotskyist – was enemy number one for Santamaria. But his fears went far deeper than that. He had with spectacular scorn denounced in his memoirs the yet unfinished revolution of the 1960s. Santamaria deplored the Pill, homosexuality, rampant materialism, married women in the workforce, environmentalists, drugs, abortion, anarchy on campuses, economic rationalism, dissident theologians, divorce without proof of guilt and the cult of the moral autonomy of the individual. What he saw at stake here was the authority of family, church and state, indeed legitimate authority in every field of life. The fear was a new Dark Age coming out of the universities. The precedent was Paris in 1968. To blame were:

The present crop of professors, lecturers, teachers, journalists, politicians, bureaucrats, media experts, bankers, and – I regret to say it – not a few of the clergy, in other words, the people who actually run society.

Young Abbott took all that on board. The question is: how much has he jettisoned since? Communism is utterly beaten and only frantic nutters fear revolution these days. Abbott is not one of them. He never shared his master's asceticism, nor his profound pessimism. But Abbott's years in the service of this strange Catholic warrior mark him to this day. Like Santa, he is not driven by money. He's not a social climber or a snob. He's never lost the protégé's sense of being on a mission, an essentially religious mission in a secular world. Western civilisation is in flux. Society is fragile. Extraordinary forces are in play. The world according to Abbott may not be in the immediate danger Santamaria feared, but it is heading the wrong way. That is the nature of things. From Santamaria he took values rather than policies, values and attitudes beyond the ordinary reach of conservatism in this country. He would emerge from the Santamaria years as a politician interrogating the drift of the world.

After a summer in Western Australia spent surfing, carousing in pubs and selling pots door to door, Abbott turned up at Monash University in January 1977 for his first AUS conference determined to fight the good fight and make a name for himself. In both he exceeded his own high expectations. A wilderness of factions were in play, factions often controlled, as the Democratic Clubs were, from beyond the university gates. The right's determination to control or crush AUS had been revitalised by the students' decision a few years earlier to support the Palestine Liberation Organisation. The anti-PLO campaign brought together the Liberals, the right of the Labor Party, the National Union of Jewish Students and Santamaria's people. It proved to be the training ground of a new cohort of leaders on both sides of politics: Abbott, Peter Costello, Eric Abetz, Michael Yabsley, Michael Danby, Michael Kroger, Nick Sherry and, a little later, Julia Gillard.

Abbott was asked by the *Weekend Australian* to write an account of the conference that appeared under a banner headline:

I ACCUSE
Phoney student thugs
Use spit and abuse
To create terror ...
By TONY ABBOTT

In his eyes, this "tragic farce" was a time of scuffles in corridors, angry confrontation, factional bastardry – always of the left – fear, provocation, systemic danger and facile causes in which nothing of any consequence was achieved.

> Generally the air was heavy with the not-unpleasant odour of mari-
> juana. The conference hall was gaily decked with gaudy Maoist flags
> and communist slogans.
> Some delegates wore badges cheerfully urging the "smashing" of
> Fraser and the shooting of Kerr. Books on sale covered everything
> one wanted to know about abortion, street fighting, subverting uni-
> versities, indoctrinating the young, and homosexuality.

These thousands of words – ending with a pure Santamaria flourish about the great risks these influences posed to "those who will eventually lead society" – were Abbott's debut in mainstream journalism. Whether his account was fair or wildly exaggerated is by now impossible to judge. What matters – and what infuriated his opponents – was that at the age of nineteen Abbott was writing with such ease and authority. His name was everywhere as the battle raged for control of AUS. He had found a public voice. He was making his mark. But these wild times and all they promised for his future seemed suddenly about to end.

His girlfriend, Kathy McDonald, was three months pregnant. It was the old Catholic catastrophe: no chastity, no contraception, no abortion and, it would turn out, no marriage. They were lovers at school, having met at a high tea for Riverview boys and Monte Sant' Angelo girls in Year 11. The *Bulletin* would report:

> She was infatuated immediately, dazzled by this intellectually pre-
> cocious, outrageously funny, albeit conservative seventeen-year-old
> boy who could quote Shakespeare and recite the great poets – and
> not always just for effect ... "We were both confident, out there
> people and we adored each other."

The affair between the Catholic rugger-bugger and the sweet lefty art student was a complex business. "I loved uni," Abbott would later say. "Having the romance with Kathy was all part of the magnificent, exuber-ant boisterous time." But he had not abandoned the notion of one day serving his church. "I was sorta wrestling with this idea of the bloody priesthood, and I kept saying, 'No, no! No sex! Against the rules!' Then I'd say, 'Oh, all right.'" A priest took McDonald aside at some point and urged her not to get in the way of Tony's vocation. As it happens she had also practised Vatican roulette once or twice with her flatmate Bill Kensell. But neither McDonald nor Abbott doubted, when she discovered she was pregnant, that the child was Tony's.

He would excoriate himself decades later for being callow, insensitive and psychologically unprepared for marriage. But many an unwilling Catholic boy had found himself at the altar at the age of nineteen. At first Abbott was going to marry her but then he pulled back. Marriage would not only rule out the priesthood but also his more immediate ambition to win the Rhodes Scholarship. There was a tradition of rugby players from Sydney going on to Oxford and his footy mates were saying to him: "Abbo, you ought to think of going for the Rhodes." But the scholarship was open only to single men. Abbott called the shots. "I decided that Kathy and I were not going to get married and that adoption was the right thing to happen." They split up in the seventh month of her pregnancy. She said: "I wanted him ... to be a white knight on a charger and fix it up for me, but he couldn't so I ended the relationship." Abbott came to the hospital in July 1977 and held the child for a few minutes before the boy was given away. "I just wasn't ready for it."

Abbo had a great season on the football field that winter, even playing a few games as tighthead prop for the university firsts. He was no longer living at St John's. That place is a paradise for men like him but he was gone after only a year and the college has never much celebrated his successes. A decision had been made that Tony was spending too much time in the pub. Now he was back home with his parents in Killara but spending long hours on the campus playing football and politics.

Santamaria's strategy was to starve student bodies of funds so cash did not fall into dangerous hands. Every student at Sydney University had to pay $10 a year to the SRC. That posed enough risks, but each SRC across Australia then delivered $2.50 of that into the hands of AUS, which meant about $700,000 a year was available for leftist causes. The plan pursued by Democratic Clubs and their allies on the campuses was first to make SRC fees voluntary, and then to cut their links with AUS. There would then be little or nothing to spend in ways Abbott attacked week after week in the *Democrat*:

> When AUS champions the women's movement; homosexual liberation; the anti-Uranium campaign and anti-Kerr campaign, it is moving beyond the scope of unionism. Whatever their merits, these causes are quite divorced from the real needs of students.

According to the roneoed flyers he and his friends were handing around the campus, there was trouble brewing everywhere in universities: gays, strikes, sit-ins, the debauching of academic standards by Marxist lecturers, Palestine, abortion, the financial woes of AUS Travel and continued disrespect shown to the man who sacked Gough Whitlam. It had to stop. The first great political campaign of Abbott's life – which he would pursue by one means or another for nearly thirty years – was to drain the money from university politics.

His plan was to win the presidency of the SRC and collapse it from above. He was well underway. In May, he had taken control of the campus

Liberal Club. It was Joe Bullock's idea: "I said we need a banner to fight under. We've got to have something that can draw people to us. The Labor Club was extreme left. There was no chance of knocking it off. But the Liberal Club was a dreadful bunch of dilettantes and social climbers. And there were not many of them. So I said: 'Let's knock off the Liberal Club.' But Tony was really reluctant. 'Oh, no, I don't want to join the Liberal Club.' He made it clear his loyalties were to Labor. Eventually I persuaded him against his better judgment to join."

All reports agree: 1977 was a terrible year. After a meeting in August at Ku-ring-gai College of Advanced Education Abbott was charged with indecent and common assault. Helen Wilson, a trainee teacher, was at the microphone defending AUS. She heard someone shout, "Why don't you smile, honey?" and says she then felt a hand groping between her legs. "I jumped back, turned around, and saw Tony Abbott laughing about two feet away. The people in the audience began laughing and jeering." Abbott would give the court a different version and produce a number of witnesses to support him: "She was speaking about me in a highly critical way, calling me an AUS basher and noted right-wing supporter. To let her know I was standing behind her I leaned forward and tapped her on the back, about the level of her jeans belt." The charges would be dismissed early in the new year but they were still hanging over him as he went into the university election season and lost – to a woman – his campaign for the presidency of the SRC.

Barbara Ramjan beat him hands down. She was of the left but her work as the SRC's welfare officer made her a popular figure on the campus. The night her victory was declared, the SRC offices saw wild scenes of bad-boy behaviour: flashing, mooning, jeering and abuse. Abbott watched all this. His loss was a very public disappointment, one of the first defeats of his life that really mattered, one he would remember for a long time. He approached Ramjan. She thought he was coming over to congratulate her. "But no, that's not what he wanted. He came up to within an inch of my nose and punched the wall on either side of my head." Thirty-five years later she recalls with cold disdain what he did. "It was done to intimidate." Abbott tells me he has no recollection of the incident: "It would be profoundly out of character had it occurred."

Abbo and his mates reckoned people just took things the wrong way. Pranks and larks. A bit of sport with humourless people. Just a game. "At times it was all rather childish," Abbott confessed years later. "At times it was a little bit scary. But it was always bloody good fun." Ramjan doesn't let him off so lightly. "He was the most in your face. That's what set him apart. There were, of course, other Liberal Party and DLP types on campus but they weren't offensive and they weren't rude. They were people you could talk to. You could sit down and have a cup of tea with them. I would never do that with Tony Abbott. He's not that sort of person. I don't care what your politics are, you can still engage with another person. You don't have to be threatening. You don't have to be just that awful person. I have no doubt Tony was a most charming man when he wanted to be. It was a very conscious choice he made." She called the year that followed – with her as president and Abbott on the SRC executive – the worst of her life. "I doubt there would have been any moment in that year that he would have been charming towards me."

But Abbott's noisy behaviour and hard-line views were winning him a following. And he was learning some political lessons. He didn't have to be a nice guy. He didn't have to go with the flow. It was possible to stand against the political tide. But where would it take him? Tyro journalist Malcolm Turnbull covered Abbott's second AUS conference for the *Bulletin*. He wrote:

> The leading light of the right-wingers in NSW is twenty-year-old
> Tony Abbott. He has written a number of articles on AUS in the
> *Australian* and his press coverage has accordingly given him a stature
> his rather boisterous and immature rhetoric doesn't really deserve.

AUS was on its last legs. Its income had nearly halved. Eleven campuses had seceded. AUS Travel had collapsed among allegations of corruption.

Turnbull acknowledged the growing support on campuses for the Democratic Clubs and for Abbott, and asked a question he must look back on now with rather grim irony: how can a student of Abbott's views hope to be a national leader?

> While he can win support from students because of the shocking state of affairs in AUS, he cannot take the next step because of his conservative moral views. Abbott is opposed to any legalisation of homosexuality and generally presents an old-fashioned DLP image. The students may be more conservative than they were a few years ago, but they have not swung back to the right as much as that.

One night that winter of 1978, the Sydney police ambushed a demonstration in Kings Cross, bashing and arresting lesbians and gay men. The paddy wagons were followed back to Darlinghurst police station by angry demonstrators. Arrests continued. One policeman dragged an unconscious woman by her hair through the station door. Four or five beat a young man's head against the station's iron gates. A woman was hit hard in the face as she sat in the dock. A man in the cells was beaten so badly he was taken, after some hours, to St Vincent's Hospital. By dawn, fifty-three men and women had been charged. As a wave of outrage swept the community, the SRC executive carried a motion unanimously condemning the "unprovoked and unnecessary police violence" and declaring: "this SRC actively supports and promotes equal rights for all lesbians and male homosexuals." The minutes explain how unanimity was achieved: "Abbott was out of room." He returned to cast a lone vote against the SRC's decision to send its protest to the NSW premier.

Abbott's name was scrawled on lavatory walls. He was attacked in Honi Soit as an extremist, fascist, careerist, parasite and stooge of the NCC. But in September 1978 he had the first real victory of his career when he finally won the presidency of the SRC. At this point he was also president of the Democratic Club, still in control of the Liberal Club and had been elected (unopposed) to sit the following year as a student fellow on the university senate. But the SRC presidency was the office that mattered and he won it without being less than himself: bully and charmer, speaker and propagandist, hard-line advocate and tireless organiser. He could usually count on the St John's crowd, though things sometimes went awry. Peter Costello recalled in his memoirs addressing an anti-AUS meeting at Sydney University:

> Tony settled on a plan to get his college mates to vote with me. He would assemble them at a nearby hotel for beer and then lead them en masse to the rally. But as the afternoon wore on, the beer proved far more compelling than the rally. They never made it. The vote was lost.

In the SRC election of 1978 Abbott campaigned hard around the conservative faculties of engineering and medicine. He called on the footy crowd to back him. "We used to go along to watch him for sport," one recalls. "He was extremely right-wing at a time when everyone was extremely left-wing. He used to bait them, particularly lesbians. There were a lot of lesbians about then." He addressed the men's colleges. He boasts of earning an ovation at St John's by promising to tear down the posters of Che Guevara at the SRC and replace them with portraits of the Queen and the Pope. He convened rowdy meetings on the university lawn. He heckled and he dealt with hecklers. He was not afraid of losing skin in the game. For the rest of his career there would be skin everywhere.

He was president, but almost alone. On a council of thirty members, he had no more than three or four supporters. He didn't build alliances; he fell out with the moderates; he created and dramatised division. He didn't like the SRC and made no secret of being happy to see it bankrupt. "I can't recall a constructive policy for the benefit of the student body that he ever put forward," says a distinguished Sydney lawyer active in university politics then. "My lasting impression is of negativity and destruction. For those he did get on with, he was well liked. He also generated an enormous amount of hostility verging on vitriolic hatred from those who were his political opponents."

They tried to prevent him taking office. The farce that followed involved police, rival teams of locksmiths, mobs of angry students, lawyers and university officials. Abbott's car aerial was snapped. He slept in his office under siege. He tried to fire SRC staff. Even those on the executive supporting his right to take office thought his behaviour "senseless, futile and provocative." This battle didn't take up all his time. The *Sydney Morning Herald* revealed in the middle of this madness that the "newly elected president of the Sydney University Students' Representative Council, Mr Tony Abbott" had joined the British morals campaigner Mrs Mary Whitehouse on the platform of a rowdy Festival of Light rally in Sydney Square to protest abortion, child porn and the permissive society. Pies and cream cakes were thrown. The *Herald* reported the Reverend Fred Nile "escaped with cream in his hair." No pies hit Abbott.

The NSW Equity Court confirmed his election a few days later and he took command of his office, waging war on graffiti, tearing down political posters, banning homosexual activists from reception, cheerfully calling the welfare officers "sluts" and berating SRC staff by name in the pages of *Honi Soit*. Abbott was running a one-man campaign to wreck his own organisation. Week after week he attacked the SRC in the student paper. The writing is sharp, fearless and provocative. One week he took readers on a tour of the SRC offices:

> Luckily, it is lunchtime, so we are able to watch a meeting of the SRC women's collective (men from a distance, as only women are allowed into the "women's" room). Grim faced, overall-clad, hard, strident, often lustfully embracing in a counterfeit of love ...

He invaded the Women's Room with a Channel Ten news crew and cub reporter Mike Munro. The issue was voluntary fees. The point was ridicule. When asked to leave the room, Abbott declared for the cameras: "This is a man's room for the moment." On ABC *Nationwide* he was calling for the slashing of both university funding and student numbers. This was to be done in the name of restoring academic rigour to Australian universities by denying Marxist lecturers the wherewithal to teach, for instance, the politics of lesbianism. He was spouting pure Santamaria: "Marxists realised that the universities now play a crucial role in the education of the elite of modern society, and they understand if they destroy the academic standards, and perhaps even the moral standards of that elite, well then they have perhaps fundamentally and fatally undermined liberal democratic society."

His footy mates loved him. "Shut up, Abbo," they'd say when he started talking politics. "Shut up, Abbo," was a familiar, affectionate taunt on the field and in the pub. They loved the daredevil in him. They forgave him his outrages. He was an affectionate and demonstrative friend. He wasn't on a mission with them. At about fifteen stone he was much bigger than he is now, a good front rower, playing in the university seconds and thirds with occasional games for the firsts when their star props were touring with the Wallabies. The rugby crowd had no idea Abbo was still thinking of the priesthood. They should have kept a closer eye on Honi Soit, which ran the SRC president's address to new students in Orientation Week, 1979:

> All physical objects, all human works are quite insubstantial in the parade of eternity – only God endures. In all ages progressive thinkers have announced the death of God. My friends, He has made more comebacks than Mohammed Ali. For most of us, he refuses to die. This is the FUNDAMENTAL TRUTH that has been forgotten by the university in its rush to be fashionable ...

Abbott organised a referendum of students in the middle of that year to decide whether Sydney University should cut its ties with AUS and whether fees for the SRC should become voluntary. The first vote passed handsomely and the second lost heavily. Abbott did not give up. He put all his efforts into persuading the university senate to defy the vote and use its own authority to decide the issue of SRC fees. This was the young man's idea of liberal democracy. He told his fellow senators: "The SRC is unnecessary and superfluous." The senators turned him down. Next he haggled over old provisions for conscientious objection to paying the fees. Who would be exempt? He demanded guarantees in writing that anyone who opposed the SRC funding "the Active Defence of Homosexuals on campus" should not have to pay fees. The senators gave no guarantee.

While he was battling this out, he stood for re-election to the senate, striking a heroic pose on the campus as a man of high principle who had "trodden an individual and even provocative course" that had to be understood in the light of his urgent purpose:

> Otherwise high-handed and precipitate actions have, I think, been justified by the potentially grave danger posed to university values and ordinary standards by certain trends on campus.

He lost – to his ally Tanya Coleman, later Costello – but like a dog with a bone didn't let the funding matter alone. He tried to persuade the senate to cut the SRC fee by $2.50, the sum no longer being sent to AUS. The motion was lost on the voices. He demanded a show of hands. It was lost again and he announced he had no option but to resign from the senate. It was not a particularly impressive gesture: this was his last meeting anyway. As he walked from the room, the chancellor, Herman Black, remarked dryly that if he wished to resign, he should do so in writing. His letter arrived three weeks later.

After a final year spent away from the political front putting his head down to study at last, he was awarded one of the great scholarships of the world: two years at Oxford courtesy of the diamond-mining fortune of Empire loyalist Cecil Rhodes. For Anglophiles and rugby players, the Rhodes was died-and-gone-to-heaven time. Winners must be scholars fond of sport who display "moral force of character and instincts to lead." The award to Abbott came as a surprise, particularly to those who had seen him up close on the SRC. One jibe at the time was: "Second-grade footballer, third-rate academic and fourth-class politician." But Abbott impressed a panel of worthies chaired by the governor of New South Wales, Sir Roden Cutler. That's what mattered. Abbott used the announcement in the *Sydney Morning Herald* to have another whack at student funds being spent on the "extreme causes" of opposing Kerr, Fraser and uranium.

He arrived in London in late summer to find himself at home. "It belonged to me," he wrote in *Battlelines*, "as much as to any Briton." And then there was Oxford. Here, at the age of twenty-three, he could be exactly who he wanted to be without being constrained by the weight of expectations placed on him for so long. Oxford had magic, not least the magic of power. "I loved my time at Oxford, I really did," he would tell ABC *Grandstand* thirty years later. "I loved the rugby. I loved my studies. I loved the opportunity to mix with a remarkable group of people from all over the world and, yes, I loved the boxing."

PUPPY LOVE: CANBERRA, 26 JUNE 2012

"Where are the animals?" David Speers asks as he climbs out of the Sky News car. It's cold at the dog pound on the outskirts of Canberra where the press pack is gathering for today's attack on the carbon tax. I give Speers the lie of the land. In the office is a woman with a white rat called Bijou on her shoulder. Out the back, a pit bull bitch called Yserah is waiting for the leader of the Opposition. They see a lot of pit bull pups at the RSPCA, her handler tells me. Why? "Because young guys have pit bulls and they are idiots and they don't desex their dogs." A sign on Yserah's empty cage says the bitch is "Zealous."

We have been to so many of these carbon tax outings over the last two and a half years. Abbott's office digs into its database, issues another "media alert" and out the press heads to another outfit about to be ruined by the Great Big Tax on Everything that has lately morphed into the Toxic Tax Based on a Lie. Six months ago there were rumblings in the party that the strategy was exhausted. But to the delight of the leader's office – and the exasperation of Labor – these jaunts are still putting Abbott's face on the news. Mind you, something of the fun has gone out of them since the time when we never knew what strange body-hugging gear Abbott might be wearing. Not anymore. His minders – and perhaps his wife – have said no to Speedos and Lycra. Even so it can be said that never in the political annals of this country have so many seen so much of so little.

The mood is perky. The dog pound promises better pictures than another visit to Bill Lilley Mitsubishi of Crawford Street, Queanbeyan. We're still waiting for Abbott to pop in to help with something a little more complicated than greasing a wheel nut or ironing a shirt. Maybe a hip replacement. Gathered in the car park are reporters from AAP, the *Australian*, the *Canberra Times* and the *Sydney Morning Herald* plus Paul Bongiorno and his crew from Ten and Speers of Sky News. Over by the gate, a woman with purple hair is climbing into a chicken suit. Her placard is lying on the ground:

The sky isn't falling!
Carbon Price = Good for Jobs
& our future!

Abbott and Greg Hunt unpack themselves from a Commonwealth car. Abbott is spotless. He walks as though he has to will each leg forward. It's curious in a man who is so obviously fit. His face is skin and bone. He smiles but his eyes are hooded. The overall effect is faintly menacing, as if he's about to climb into the ring. Bijou is presented to him as he crosses the foyer. His response is faultless. Patting the little rodent, he says: "I suppose I should show my professional respects."

The press has given up saying so but these two men are denouncing what they once supported: a price on carbon and an emissions trading scheme. Here is Hunt, the Opposition spokesman on climate change who wrote his final-year thesis at Melbourne University in 1990 on the benefits of countering global warming by taxing polluters. And here is Abbott, whose support for emissions trading helped persuade John Howard his government should take that course. All that's changed is the politics. From the moment he became leader of the Opposition Abbott has driven a scare campaign to convince us this tax will destroy the economy. He's done so with flair and immense determination. But Abbott's wild hyperbole is about to be tested. The tax is only days away.

Yserah has vanished. "I was told I wasn't allowed to use a pit bull," says her rather baffled handler, for at the end of her lead now is Mars Bar, a beautiful young Rottweiler. What's the difference? As it happens, the press pack is not going to crack jokes today about attack-dog politicians. The cameras barely record the self-confessed junkyard dog's encounter with the Rottweiler and get to work only as the politicians begin to cuddle a couple of part Staffy puppies, Gloves and Mittens. The names had been chosen only that morning. They run through a lot of names at a dog pound. As the flashlights blaze Hunt mugs for the cameras: "Gorgeous, and the puppy's pretty too."

Instead of gathering in the car park we huddle among the kennels, hiding from the chicken lady. It smells like a nursing home back here. "The RSPCA is one of Australia's great charities," says Abbott once all the microphones are set. "It is a household name and justly so. It is one of the many organisations which is going to be damaged by the carbon tax." He speaks with grave regret. "I will be travelling the length and breadth of Australia in the first fortnight of the carbon tax's introduction just pointing out to people that every family's cost of living is going to be harmed. Every Australian job is going to be less secure and it is not actually going to reduce emissions."

What are we doing here? The local CEO, Michael Linke, tells us the carbon tax will cost the RSPCA $180,000 across Australia. Jobs will go. "There is absolutely no way that I'm going to compromise animal welfare." I stop him as he walks away from the microphone to ask what seems the obvious question: what's the RSPCA's national budget? "$90 million."

That night Abbott and Hunt are on television cuddling those puppies while denouncing the brutal impact of the carbon tax on the RSPCA. There are a few clips of Julia Gillard's mockery in the House: "I can tell the Leader of the Opposition, on the first of July, cats will still purr, dogs will still bark and the Australian economy will continue to get strong." Next morning the Sydney Morning Herald shows Abbott petting the rat. (Typical.) Over the next days, the RSPCA deals with a storm of criticism for taking part in this political exercise. Animal lovers are assured the RSPCA supports action on climate change. Gloves and Mittens find a home.

FATHERS AND SON

In the subdivisions of Emu Plains, Tony Abbott came to doubt his vocation. He was nearly thirty. He had spent two unhappy years in a seminary and ordination was still years away. In summer at the foot of the Blue Mountains he found himself teaching scripture to kids, running a youth group and occasionally preaching at Our Lady of the Way. A spiritual apprenticeship in the suburbs was not, he wrote, without its rewards. "But I found it difficult to believe that this was meant to be my life."

Another strange mentor was responsible for this detour, another of the men offering him a borderline cause to follow, another he fell for head over heels: "I doubt that I have ever met a finer man than Paul Mankowski." They remain in close contact. The Jesuit is now a controversial figure in his order, much distrusted for pursuing beyond the grave a hero of the Catholic left: Father Bob Drinan, an anti-war, pro-choice Jesuit who sat in Congress for a decade until ordered out by John Paul II. That Washington crisis was coming to a head when Abbott and Mankowski met in the boxing world at Oxford. The priest recruited him first to the ring – Abbott's four wins in four fights earned him two blues and a fine reputation as a boxing dervish – and then persuaded him to enter the priesthood. The idea had never entirely left him and Mankowski was just the figure to revive this old ambition. He was a younger, more fascinating Emmet Costello: "both the embodiment of muscular Christianity and fully acquainted with the cross tides of modern life." Under Mankowski's spell, Abbott came home in 1984 determined to give the priesthood a go. But this was never a simple exercise in piety.

Why enter St Patrick's Seminary at Manly? Why not study for the priesthood in England or Rome? Why not the Jesuits? "He wanted to be Archbishop of Sydney," says Father Michael Kelly, a confidant at the time. It was not an ignoble ambition but ahead of Abbott lay a long and celibate road. His sisters were put out. "We were all just horrified, because we felt the priesthood was not the career for him," said his sister Jane Vincent.

They believed him destined for politics. "It's what he's cut out for. It suits his character, and the way he's been brought up ... he's exactly the right sort of person to be prime minister." But Abbott was determined. He was an amazing "get" for the church: footballer, student leader and Rhodes Scholar. "Tony came to the seminary a brilliant young fellow," recalled the president of St Patrick's, Dr Grove Johnson. "He came in with all of the fervour, the driving ambition – in a good sense – to make himself of service." One of his teachers was the historian Father Edmund Campion: "He wasn't so much a big fish in a small pond as a whale in a swimming pool. People felt swamped by his intellectual achievements and by the force of his personality."

He didn't disappear from view. To the surprise of old adversaries at Sydney University, a gentler Tony was explaining himself in the pages of the *Australian* only a few weeks after entering the seminary:

> As time went by it seemed to me the real issues were not so much political but spiritual; the important arena was not Parliament, the economy or the strategic balance but the human heart; the great qualities were not ambition, ability or eloquence but love. It's been said I have a martyr complex, that I like to rush off and engage in heroic struggles for lost causes. I hope that's not true. We humans have something very deep in us which is repelled by the idea of God. I think that's our pride and the Christian is in a sense constantly at war with the world and often at war with himself.

To his dismay, Abbott found himself in an institution as confused, often vapid and unsure of itself as Sydney University had been. Once again, authority was under attack. This time the trouble-makers weren't Marxists but theologians at war with the Vatican. The place was too camp for his taste, too gay. There was too much navel-gazing. He was much older than his class, much brighter and more a man of the world. He quickly loathed the place. Things grew worse in his second year when Dr Johnson was replaced by a man with new-fangled, superficially democratic ideals and deep belief in what Abbott took to be psychobabble.

"Tony wasn't one to walk on the headland with beads in his hands," says Noel Debien, an ABC broadcaster and fellow St Patrick's seminarian. "He was not a meditator. He loved good music and was moved by ceremony. But he was impatient with frippery. He was not one of the squeaky-black-shoes and soutane brigade. He was orthodox and straightforward. His attitude was: 'Tell me what's required and I'll do it. I do not need to go on a fucking *journey*.' He took it all so seriously. Tony didn't warm to the very black, camp sense of humour in the place, a way of dealing with the difficulties of it all. It was difficult. Celibacy is hard. It is not an easy thing to be in the prime of your life and you can't even wank."

Abbott couldn't help himself: he took the problems of St Patrick's to the press. An article for the *Catholic Weekly* was never published but a letter appeared in the *Northern Herald* explaining why so many seminarians dropped out:

> St Patrick's is a microcosm of the Church where the tensions only too evident in contemporary Catholicism are brought into sharp and often painful focus. This is the central reality of St Patrick's ... the real reason for the drop-out rate ... include ennui, psychosomatic illness and unwillingness to conform to whatever model of priesthood happens to be momentarily fashionable.

The letter was a bold move, says Debien. "Talking to the press was a sign you had given up on the church. I thought he was a hero. He was pressing the self-destruct button but thank God someone was saying this stuff."

The cardinal was furious. Abbott was swiftly in Emu Plains. After a few months out by the mountains he was shifted to North Rocks, closer to the city. All this time he was negotiating the terms of a return to the seminary. A way was eventually found but he'd had enough. At football training on Sydney University oval – he had been coaching since his return from England – he announced he was quitting. The response was enthusiastic and ribald. Abbott wrote in the *Bulletin*:

Three years' grinding struggle to meet the Church's standard was over. But a dream had died, as well – the dream that I could join that splendoured company founded by Christ which has angered, amazed and enthralled the world ever since.

The many accounts he has given of the death of this dream make it clear the fundamental issue wasn't celibacy – though surely that would have become impossible in time – but the bleak conviction that "serving a local church at a time of disillusion and decline" wasn't worth the sacrifice. The power of Rome was in question; the authority of the priesthood was in doubt; and the modern church was deliberately downplaying its own mystique. What was the point of giving up so much for so long – perhaps twenty years – to become a bishop in a church that had abandoned its heroic mission? It was a prospect of little power and no glory.

Besides, what might have dawned on Abbott a decade earlier was now becoming clear: what really interested him was politics. Labor had been making overtures to him while he was still in the seminary. Bob Carr tried once or twice. In the end, Abbott wasn't interested. Sometimes he would say he disapproved of union control, sometimes that he didn't like the party's republicanism. No young man of ambition would bother with the DLP, smashed by Gough Whitlam in the 1970s. That left the Liberals. Bob Santamaria didn't like his people joining the toffs' party, but that's where conservative professional Catholics were drifting. Sometime soon after he left St Patrick's, Abbott made an appointment to see the leader of the Opposition, John Howard.

Abbott was not joking when he called himself Howard's "political love child." About to lose an election that had been his to win, under siege from both his deputy and the corrupt premier of Queensland, Joh Bjelke-Petersen, the beleaguered John Howard would be the young man's next great mentor. Abbott would owe each step in his political career for the next twenty years to this man. Howard was entranced from the start. He had done his homework. He knew this was the former student politician, the footballer, the Rhodes Scholar, the ex-seminarian. He found him "Very intelligent, easy to talk to, had a lot of views the same as me; was traditional about a lot of things, but he was also somebody with a great enquiring mind ... he saw Australia as something of an outpost of Western civilisation and values in the Asian Pacific region, and having to combine the history and the geography of our country, which he thought we could do ... I thought he had real political talent." There was a vague offer of a job – sometime.

Abbott worked at the *Bulletin*. Next door at the Kings Head Tavern one night he met Margaret Aitken, a New Zealander working for the Rothschild bank. She would never forget him taking her aside on their first date to explain the ins and outs of the Split. She liked the man but never really warmed to politics. Emmet Costello married them the following year. After a brief interregnum managing a concrete plant for Tristan Antico, Abbott followed his old *Bulletin* editor David Armstrong to the *Australian* to write editorials. Abbott joined the union, the Australian Journalists' Association. He led a little strike at the *Bulletin* and opposed a big strike at the *Australian*. "He would make aggressive speeches at meetings," recalls Alan Kennedy. "I think he saw himself carrying the Santamaria banner into battle against us commos." That's when journalists began calling him, among themselves, the Mad Monk.

Howard lost the leadership in 1989 and Bob Hawke beat the Coalition for the fourth time in March 1990. Soon afterwards, at this nadir in the fortunes of the Liberal Party, Abbott had lunch with Howard. There was a job going: the latest leader of the Opposition needed a press secretary. Abbott was in Canberra twenty-four hours later. "I was attracted by his intellect, his doggedness, his passion and his conviction," said John Hewson. But it was a brave appointment to make. They were very different men. Later on Abbott would say he was a Catholic idealist serving a Baptist technocrat workaholic. But in the early days, Abbott was deeply impressed:

He had called his advisers together, and we were talking about the coming couple of years leading up to the 1993 election, and John said something like this: losing an election would not be the end of the world, but going to an election without a policy, or a set of policies, that I really believed in – *that* would be the real failure.

Now I was thrilled to hear this, and I thought to myself, in the tradition of B.A. Santamaria, this is a *man*, not a political weathervane. Whether you like him or dislike him, whether you support his policies or not, this is a *man* in politics.

But Hewson didn't use Abbott's speeches and didn't much value his advice. He was not in the inner circle. And he was learning his job from scratch. Abbott was an opinion writer, not a reporter. He had no contacts in and no experience dealing with the Canberra press gallery. It didn't help that both men were instinctively wary of the press. Alan Ramsey wrote:

> In twenty-five years in Canberra, I remember no Opposition leader who blitzed the press gallery boxes with as many pieces of paper as does Hewson. His office churns them out at a furious pace, often pages in length. Yet the gallery hardly ever gets to talk to the man behind the words.

This is when I first met Abbott. *Four Corners* was doing a profile of Hewson. Standard stuff. But Abbott was demanding the impossible: all questions in writing in advance. We refused. The result was a mess that didn't play well for Hewson. The press gallery was whingeing about a press secretary "who keeps very close counsel indeed." The nickname Mad Monk became public currency.

The most important task Abbott performed for Hewson was turning *Fightback!* into prose. Hewson's Australia was to have a goods and services tax and Hewson's impeccable approach was to stage a year's debate before putting the tax to the people at the coming election. *Fightback!* was the end of Hawke. Within weeks Paul Keating was prime minister and hard at work attacking this great big tax on everything, a tax which in his heart he deeply admired. Abbott gave the Labor leader useful ammunition, drafting a speech for Hewson with a few lines of Killara snobbery that would haunt the Opposition leader all the way to the ballot box and beyond:

> In any street, of course, it's always easy to tell the rented houses. They're the ones where the lawn isn't mowed, the plants aren't watered and the fences aren't fixed.

Hewson was a bad-tempered boss. Abbott handled the outbursts well but relations between them deteriorated. Hewson said: "He was one of the most interesting and challenging people on the one hand, and one of the most frustrating people I've ever met in my life." In February 1992 he shunted Abbott aside, leaving him with the vague task of looking after "political and communications strategy in the lead-up to the election." Abbott wouldn't go. He needed the job: his second and third daughters were born while he worked for Hewson. The great consolation in these difficult years was growing closer to Howard. This increased the tension in Hewson's office. "While I always knew that he was running his own and Howard's race," said Hewson, "I was never really sure when he was running mine." Abbott tried to get out. He applied to be director of the NSW Liberal Party but Barry O'Farrell got the job. Abbott would depart, come what may, after the 1993 election, which Hewson seemed bound to win. The two men fell out finally after this shocking loss when Hewson, determined to remain leader of the party, announced he would ditch *Fightback!* Abbott wrote him a memo: "How can you sacrifice your principles to save your job, when you would not sacrifice your principles to save the election?"

Abbott cites this exchange with Hewson in 1993 as a clarifying moment in his career. Deep convictions frankly expressed had made his boss unelectable. More finesse was required. He told Santamaria loyalists gathered in late 2008 at a dinner for their newspaper, *News Weekly*, that this didn't necessarily mean abandoning principles. "If you don't have them, what is the point of life in politics?" But principles must be pursued "intelligently and sensitively" so as not to frighten the public:

> The art of effective democratic statesmanship is of presenting your principles, presenting your convictions, in ways which sufficiently impress the public such that you are seen as a man or woman of principle, but which don't so worry the public that they think you would be a risk if you found yourself in a position of power.

Since witnessing the Hewson catastrophe at first hand, Abbott has worn a mask. He has grown and changed. Life and politics have taught him a great deal. But how this has shaped the fundamental Abbott is carefully obscured. What has been abandoned? What is merely hidden on the road to power? It is hard to tell, especially as he continues to insist he is a politician of enduring values. What makes people so uneasy about Abbott is the sense that he is biding his time, that there is a very hard operator somewhere behind that mask, waiting for power. He came away from those years with Hewson convinced more than ever that a real *man* must win: "Unless you're in a position to make executive decisions, it is – dare I say it? – but sounding brass and tinkling cymbal."

SAFETY OF LIFE: HOUSE OF REPRESENTATIVES, 27 JUNE 2012

Out in the Indian Ocean another rescue is underway. This time Australia swiftly sent help to the stricken vessel. The last boat in trouble was left unrescued for over thirty hours as Australia tried – and inevitably failed – to persuade the Indonesians to take its cargo back again. Over ninety died. Death has brought the boats issue back to life. Question Time is suspended. Gillard is pushing Malaysia again. The Opposition is insisting the government capitulate utterly: abandon Malaysia, resume processing refugees on Nauru and defy Indonesia by forcing refugee boats back to the Java coast.

A little cohort of Liberals, long troubled by their party toying with the race fears of this country, is threatening to cross the floor. Greens and senior Liberals take the dissidents aside by turns. Julie Bishop kisses Mal Washer. It is a peck of gratitude. She has his vote. While negotiations continue in clumps around the chamber, Opposition politicians queue at the dispatch box to sing arias to human rights. Even Kevin Andrews, the jailer of Dr Mohamed Haneef, is caterwauling about the vulnerable needing rights. It is an arresting, complicated and contradictory scene. Conservative politicians who have ridiculed every effort to entrench human rights protections in Australian law for fifty years are weeping in the House on behalf of Hazaras and Tamils who would be left unprotected if dispatched to Malaysia.

"We have always believed in offshore processing with protections," intones Abbott. Not quite. As if rising from the grave, John Howard's old immigration minister Philip Ruddock gets to his feet to remind the House that it was Labor that insisted during the *Tampa* crisis that fundamental human rights be incorporated in the Pacific Solution. "This matter turns on the very question of whether or not you walk away from those obligations on offshore processing now. We are seeking … no more than Kim Beazley demanded of us at that time."

Abbott is looking particularly earnest as he faces the cameras later in the gardens of parliament. Each sentence comes with a reflective little pause. "We did try hard today to reach what we thought was a principled compromise." This is risible. He had held his rebels in check by promising to increase the quota of refugees an Abbott government would take. Nothing more. Earlier in the day he had spoken of consulting his conscience. There is none of that now. He bats press questions away, hardly pretending to address them. He knows there is no guarantee Nauru will work. He knows boats can't be towed back. He knows that unless the big parties can come to some agreement, the Greens will block both their plans in the Senate. The stalemate he brought us out here to condemn is his work as much as anyone's. This is a happy man with a grave face.

WikiLeaks told us how keen the Coalition is to exploit the boats. In late 2009, in the dying days of Malcolm Turnbull's leadership of the Opposition, a "key Liberal party strategist" popped in to the US embassy in Canberra to say how pleased the party was that refugee boats were, once again, making their way to Christmas Island. "The issue was 'fantastic,'" he said. "And 'the more boats that come the better.'" But he admitted they had yet to find a way to make the issue work in their favour: "his research indicated only a 'slight trend' towards the Coalition."

Abbott found the way. That Christ himself was a refugee doesn't trouble him one bit. He has a Jesuitical line he offers troubled constituents that is almost too embarrassing to put down in black and white: the flight into Egypt took the Holy Family to the nearest sanctuary. Hazaras, by contrast, are reaching Australia via Indonesia. If Mary, Joseph and Jesus had gone to Babylon, it might be a different matter. As it is, Abbott's Christian conscience sees nothing standing in the way of taking political advantage of boat people. The slight trend has become a mighty swing in the Coalition's favour – once again. In the Abbott analysis, Howard saved his skin by stopping the boats. The argument goes something like this: Howard won the battlers in '96, almost lost them in '98 with the GST but enough stayed around to let him squeak home. Then he won them all back in '01 with strong border protection.

Abbott cast himself as a hero in the battle of the boats. The old derogatory rhetoric was deployed with fresh aggression: Australia was under invasion; Australia had lost control of its borders; Labor lacked the will to protect the nation; Labor was "rolling out the red carpet" for these "illegals." Compassion is "moral vanity." Abbott even mused one morning on Perth radio that it was un-Christian for refugees to come by sea. He licensed his immigration spokesman, Scott Morrison, to link boat people with exotic diseases, the drug trade and gun-running. At one point he faced open revolt in his party after backing Morrison's complaints about money spent flying survivors of a boat wreck to the funerals of their families. Briefly it seemed Abbott's leadership might be under threat after a member of shadow cabinet, disgusted by what was going on, leaked to the press that Morrison had suggested the party capitalise on growing concerns about Muslim immigration. In the *Sydney Morning Herald*, Peter Hartcher reported being told: "He put it on the table like a dead cat." There was talk in the party of easing up on boat people. It was not to be. One Liberal MP told the *Courier Mail*: "It works incredibly well for us in outer metropolitan electorates."

The polls show eight out of ten Australians are anxious about the boats. Most of us want the Pacific Solution back. Most of us think Labor far too soft on boat people. This day's stalemate will be blamed, over-whelmingly, on the government. From the moment Julia Gillard became prime minister, Abbott's mantra has been: "If you want to stop the boats, you have to change the government." But for that to keep working in his favour, it's best the boats keep coming. These days they are coming in record numbers.

Someone up the back was rudely demanding the chairman say what side he was on: the crown or the republic? The hall of St John's Anglican Church in Gordon was stuffy. The heckler wouldn't let up. His question was fair but astonishingly abrupt by the standards of Sydney's upper North Shore. Malcolm Turnbull had given his spiel. Paul Keating had appointed him the day before to chair a committee of eminent Australians to advise on the shape of the republic. The rather courtly barrister Lloyd Waddy delivered his defence of the crown. As the meeting broke up, the heckler introduced himself to Waddy. "This very possessed, good-looking, solid man came out of the crowd and said: 'If you're looking for anyone to speak up for the monarchy, mate, I'm your man.'" It was Tony Abbott.

Waddy hired Abbott to run ACM, Australians for Constitutional Monarchy. "We never looked back from there. The monarchists were not being heard and he made us heard. He said to me: 'Mate, mate, we've got to set this up across Australia.' And he got the money to travel. And he got the most wonderfully representative groups of people together right across Australia: men, women, young, old, migrants." He rallied the troops, the bad cop to Waddy's good cop. He wrote a blizzard of press releases and opinion pieces for the press. "He was an absolute genius with the pen." The first killer phrase of Abbott's political career was: "the Keating republic." That he broke every preconception of what a monarchist was supposed to look like made him a particularly effective recruiting officer. He wasn't a forelock-tugging, elderly silvertail. He was this ocker.

Sentimentality and an instinctive hostility to change don't quite explain Abbott's attachment to the monarchy. He was still the incorrigible Anglophile of his childhood. No Fenian suspicions about the crown had rubbed off on him in his Catholic school days. The crown was history and heroism, romance and pageantry, one of the great institutions of Western civilisation. There is little sign in Abbott of a personal devotion to Elizabeth II, but he shared the old DLP reverence for John Kerr. Twenty-five years before he dismissed Gough Whitlam, Kerr was one of the brilliant lawyers stripping communists out of the unions for Santamaria. From the moment Abbott reached university in the months just after the sacking, defending Kerr from his detractors was a cherished cause. And now there was the raw political necessity of denying Keating a triumph. Abbott wrote: "Any republic that comes about under Keating will be Keating's republic and Keating's possession."

By the time ACM was up and running in the middle of 1993, Australia seemed to be drifting towards a republic. Half the country wanted to be rid of the crown. The political establishment was essentially republican and had been so for years. The press was republican. The rich suburbs were strongly republican. Labor, the Democrats and the Greens all officially backed the republic. More than half the Liberal caucus was personally committed to the cause. But there remained a stubborn third of the nation wedded to the crown and that would rise to a little over 40 per cent once ACM began making its mark. That is a powerful constituency. As he began putting ACM together, Abbott wrote a blistering article in the *Australian* to remind John Hewson that no issue was above politics and there were politics to be played here: he didn't have to be "relevant" and "swim with the community mood" and should he allow the Liberals even a free debate on the monarchy he risked months of "vicious infighting" that might destroy the party.

That was always the Santamaria way: when you haven't got the numbers, be vicious. It's called minority politics. Abbott would come to play them superbly, having learnt in the Democratic Club how small constituencies can cause big trouble. It's a matter of passion rather than numbers. The crucial weakness of the Australian republican movement was having not much more than reason on its side. By and large this is a country of milksop republicans. But Abbott, by engaging the anger of the minority, could turn the monarchists into a more formidable bloc than polling figures suggested possible. Walling in the crown was only the immediate aim. Across politics and across the country, the monarchists were on about something vague and big. ACM was holding the line.

Abbott claims the campaign changed him. Until his mid-thirties, he had been all for an absolutely Australian Australia, not necessarily white but true to the country Australians had always known. In 1990 he wrote: "There is no reason why a Vietnamese cannot become thoroughly Australian – provided he is encouraged to do so – rather than remain a Vietnamese who happens to be living here." In the *Australian* that day, Abbott backed Howard's right to call for a slowdown in Asian immigration; he endorsed Alfred Deakin's rationale for the White Australia policy; he wrote of Asians making true Australians "feel like an endangered species through destruction of habitat"; and he demanded immediate assimilation as the price of entry for everyone arriving here from beyond the Anglosphere:

> The issue is the sort of Australia we want our children and grand-
> children to inherit. Will it be a relatively cohesive society that stud-
> ies Shakespeare, follows cricket and honours the Anzacs; or will it
> be a pastiche of cultures with only a geographic home in common?

But then he found himself working with Greek and Italian Australians who had not shed their old allegiances. Their passion for the monarchy grew out of their own home soil. They were fighting for the crown here because they believed Greece and Italy had gone to the dogs since becoming republics. They were Abbott's kind of people. No harm to the country. It beggars belief, perhaps, but working with people like Sophie Mirabella née Panopoulos reconciled Abbott to multiculturalism. He told Paul Kelly about a decade later: "I had been altogether too ungenerous to migrants. I had it wrong and I made a mistake." But he cautioned that his idea of multiculturalism remained "very conservative."

After less than a year at the helm of ACM, Abbott had a call from John Howard. The seat of Warringah was about to fall vacant. Those waterfront suburbs – from Neutral Bay around to Middle Head and over to Manly – are among the best conservative real estate in Australia. They had not been on the market for twenty-four years. The man with the inside running would be Kevin McCann, a leading Sydney solicitor, company director and Liberal moderate. But Howard wanted one of his own in the seat. He urged Abbott to contest. The young man took a little time to consider. It was early February before his name began to appear in press lists of contenders. Though by far the most conservative man among these middle-aged professionals and failed state politicians, Tony Abbott would somehow come to represent the possibilities of a fresh start. It's a career pattern.

That he won Warringah with a single speech is a myth. Not in living memory had there been such an open, aggressive and competitive Liberal pre-selection contest as there was in Warringah in 1993. The rules had changed. Instead of fifty selectors under tight party control making the choice, the selection was now thrown open to a caucus of 200 with the rank and file having a decisive say. Abbott's referees included Laurie Oakes but most were monarchists. They included John Howard and Bronwyn Bishop, who had come down from the Senate to contest the nearby seat of Mackellar. She and her backers believed at this point that the leadership of the party was within her grasp. Santamaria saved Abbott's bacon by refusing to give him a reference. So besotted was Abbott still with the old man, he believed his backing would be a great help. In fact, it would have seemed ridiculous to the selectors of Warringah. Crucial support came from Radio 2UE's Alan Jones, who was commending the contender on air as a fine young fellow and the very best sort of Australian. At this point began one of the great unconsummated love affairs of Australian politics.

The big day in Manly was Sunday 20 February. Good performances at candidates' nights had placed Abbott among the top three contenders. As always, he was writing for newspapers in his own cause; he was on radio calling for the Liberals to become "the party of ideas"; and he distributed a video showing the good work he had done for ACM on television. Jones had written a personal letter to each of the 200 selectors. Bishop, with all the allure of a possible leader, was working the phones. Howard praised Abbott as "a very good political scrapper." That Sunday, the candidate came quietly onto the stage of the Manly Leagues Club, moved the lectern to one side and, without notes, delivered a speech full of fight, short on detail, long on pride in the Liberal Party. He ended by pledging himself to a great cause: "reclaiming our political culture and helping Australia to achieve the greatness that we all know is within our grasp." He beat McCann by sixteen votes.

His maiden speech was also lyrical and far-ranging. He did all the right things: pledge his faith in politics, commend his predecessors in Warringah and thank all those who had inspired and supported him. A long list began with his family, mentioned the Jesuits, paused to remember Santamaria "who sparked my interest in politics" and ended at the feet of "the contemporary politician I admire most," John Howard. The new man pledged to be true to them all:

> May God and the ghosts of great men give me strength. May those who have laboured greatly to build this nation fortify my resolve to make a worthy contribution in this House.

What that contribution might be was up for grabs. The day after his by-election victory, and weeks before he gave parliament this elevated job description, he told the press he was looking forward to being a "junkyard dog savaging the other side."

His own side was a mess. Hewson fell three weeks after Abbott entered parliament. Alexander Downer lasted only eight months. Howard returned like Lazarus from the grave and took the Coalition to a great victory in March 1996. But to the member for Warringah's immense frustration, the man he so revered kept failing to take him into the ministry. He believed someone of his "political horsepower" should be given a go. He had it out with the prime minister. Howard was unmoved.

Abbott discovered he'd had a traitor in the nest when a key member of his staff, David Oldfield, defected to run One Nation. This suave conservative from Manly had mustered votes for Abbott's pre-selection. His aggressive positions on migrants and Aborigines were no secret. Oldfield would say, "Abbott's concerns were the same as mine." That's been denied many times by Abbott, but whatever the differences between them, the new member for Warringah had been comfortable giving a man with such a reputation a job in his office. He went further, delivering a memorably savage attack in parliament on the reputation of Oldfield's opponent in the NSW elections of 1995. The fate of John Fahey's Liberal government depended on Oldfield winning Manly for the Liberals. He failed to do so after a bizarre and dirty campaign that saw the party having to muzzle the candidate to disguise his unpleasant views. Bob Carr took office for a decade.

Abbott and Oldfield worked closely together in the federal campaign of 1996. But before the year was out, Oldfield was plotting with the Queensland renegade Pauline Hanson to set up her new party. This emerged only after he left Abbott's office in April 1997 armed with a glowing reference from the member for Warringah. A humiliated Abbott blasted Oldfield: "He's a dangerous, snaky Rasputin who thrives on notoriety. Sure, I had him on my staff when I knew he held some unnaturally intense views on some things, but he seemed like a Liberal with a reasonable standing in the community. I'm not making any big claims for myself, but even Jesus had his Judas."

Howard was pussyfooting with Hanson. But Abbott began openly attacking her party, especially after One Nation scooped up eleven seats in the June 1998 Queensland elections delivering government to Labor's Peter Beattie. Behind the scenes Abbott was secretly assisting two court actions brought by disgruntled party members to strip One Nation of public funding. "My view was that the situation was so dire that you had to take whatever allies you could find." In early July 1998 he gave a curious figure called Terry Sharples a handwritten guarantee to cover out-of-pocket expenses from the litigation. It was grossly unwise. It exposed Abbott to the possibility of significant financial liabilities and made it impossible for him, in the end, to cover his tracks. In August, he lied to Tony Jones of *Four Corners*:

Jones: So there was never any question of any party funds –

Abbott: Absolutely not.

Jones: Or other funds from any other source –

Abbott: Absolutely not.

Jones: Being offered to Terry Sharples?

Abbott: Absolutely not.

A few weeks later Marian Wilkinson of the *Sydney Morning Herald* reported Abbott backing the second action against One Nation and setting up a shadowy trust, Australians for Honest Politics, to defray the costs. He would finally come clean to parliament about these backroom machinations – which led to Hanson being jailed in Queensland for a time – but for the rest of his career he has had to live with that lie. He didn't help matters when he told Deborah Snow of the *Sydney Morning Herald* in 2000, "Misleading the ABC is not quite the same as misleading the parliament as a political crime."

Abbott's colleagues were in awe of his savagery but worried about his judgment. The One Nation mess left many wondering how capable he was of sizing up people and causes. His public stance against Hanson earned him a good deal of admiration inside and outside the Liberal Party but also the condemnation of many of his natural allies on the political right. The Sharples dealings intensified doubts that Abbott didn't know where to draw the line. He was seen to be a bit too keen to run crusades of his own. In unattributed briefings to the press, Liberal parliamentarians were calling him the unguided missile and the loaded dog of the government. And there was also, as if designed deliberately to exacerbate these worries, his defamation case against Bob Ellis.

The portly raconteur had defamed Abbott's old university ally Tanya Coleman, who was now Tanya Costello, wife of the nation's treasurer. In *Goodbye Jerusalem*, his latest volume of political reminiscences, Ellis wrote: "Abbott and Costello were both in the Right Wing of the Labor Party till the one woman fucked both of them and married one of them and inducted them into the Young Liberals." The story was a complete canard. And by not naming her, Ellis had also managed to defame Margie Abbott. The book was withdrawn and pulped within days of publication. The publishers were willing to apologise and pay damages. But the wounded parties decided to sue. On the far side of a deeply embarrassing trial was the prospect of more money. The comic element in all this was the decision of the men to join their wives in the action against Random House. What was the slur on them? The deputy leader of the Liberal Party and its most fearless attack dog told the court their reputations had been damaged terribly by the suggestion they were so "weak and unreliable" that they would abandon their political allegiances for sex.

Abbott did a little back-burning to protect himself. A few weeks after *Goodbye Jerusalem* appeared he had his friend Christopher Pearson, the editor of the *Adelaide Review*, reveal for the first time the existence of the child born twenty years earlier. It was well done. Abbott said: "Under modern adoption laws, it's quite likely that one day someone will knock on the door and say: 'Hello, Dad.' I hope I can cope if it happens." Confession and hoped-for absolution.

The trial opened in the ACT Supreme Court a few days after Howard's 1998 victory and proved a source of national amusement. I was as guilty as anyone. There were just too many jokes about Abbott and Costello to fit on a broadsheet page. The whole thing was clearly agony for their wives but in the end this purgatory of ridicule proved financially worthwhile: the Costellos were awarded $164,000 and the Abbotts $113,500. The best joke in all those weeks was a sight gag. One afternoon Abbott and Costello were absent from this trial to make good their damaged reputations. Their seats were empty. The court had allowed them to go to Yarralumla, where Costello was sworn in once again as treasurer and Tony Abbott for the first time as Minister for Employment Services.

The Sulo factory is going flat out when the Commonwealth cars arrive at Somersby. We're all shouting over the noise of the mighty moulding machines pumping out their daily quota of wheelie bins. The machines will pause when the time comes for the leader of the Opposition to detail the impact of the toxic carbon tax on SULO MGB Australia Pty Ltd, the biggest manufacturer of mobile garbage bins in the nation. Turning out for the occasion are Joe Hockey and John Howard's former right-hand man, now senator, Arthur Sinodinos. They are enjoying themselves. We're all in Sulo's yellow fluoro vests. Hockey should travel with one of his own. The machines are heaving and pumping as Abbott begins attaching a pair of black wheels to a green bin.

He is just back from Darwin, where he had half an hour with Susilo Bambang Yudhoyono. "What will you say to him about your plan to turn back the boats to Indonesia?" David Speers had asked before Abbott flew north. He refused to answer then and is refusing to answer now. Good manners dictate discretion, he says. He will not indulge in megaphone diplomacy. Etc. It will emerge in a day or so after this jaunt to Somersby that he said nothing to Yudhoyono about the key Coalition strategy the Indonesians flatly oppose. They make that clear anyway, megaphone clear. No boats will be towed back to Indonesia. Gillard brands Abbott a coward.

Down south once more, the leader of the Opposition is facing the challenge of keeping alive the horrors of the carbon tax in the face of its undramatic debut four days ago. Not that all has been plain sailing. For days the tuneless Minister for Trade, Craig Emerson, has been singing his anti-Abbott ditty on television:

> No Whyalla wipe-out, there on my TV.
> No Whyalla wipe-out, there on my TV.
> No Whyalla wipe-out there on my TV,
> shocking me right out of my brain!

Abbott has always had a knack of sidestepping blame for his own hyperbole. Even wild exaggerations are rarely held against him. He retracts a little and is forgiven a lot. "What you've got is constant colour and movement," says his old boss John Hewson. "He gets right in your face. He exaggerates; he grabs the headlines, even if he knows that the next day he's gonna have to back that off." Abbott has been grabbing headlines about Gillard's tax for eighteen months. Now it has begun and it seems hardly anyone has noticed. For a little while Abbott was preparing for this moment by softening his rhetoric. "It's going to be a python squeeze rather than a cobra strike," he said in early June. It's a great line that went straight into the language. But as he criss-crosses the country now, attacking the tax on factory floors and in radio studios, the hyperbole is flowing as if he will never be called to account.

> It will make every job less secure ... play havoc with household budgets ... hit every Australian family's cost of living ... Every time you turn on a light, you pay. Every time you open the fridge, you pay. Every time you go to the airport or get on a bus or order a cup of coffee, you pay ... the carbon tax is going to make everything much, much worse ...

But week one of the tax reveals that Abbott and his front bench are out there alone. There is no uproar. Business is not manning the barricades. Those who hate the tax are leaving it all to Abbott and his team. Those who aren't fussed are hoping he will go away and let them get on with the inevitable. For the first time in a long time the leader of the Opposition is making himself available to heavy-hitting interviewers: Fran Kelly of ABC Radio National, Speers of Sky and Jon Faine of ABC Radio in Melbourne. He's testing himself against the best. They don't believe him when he talks crippling financial burden. Nor does the little knot of press gathered here at Somersby on the NSW Central Coast.

The machines are still, the cameras waiting and the leader of the Opposition is ready to give it another go. In politics we know repetition is everything. "This is an important local manufacturer. They are engaged in a never-ending struggle to survive and it is important that we don't make that more difficult." He tells us gravely that Gillard's tax will add $188,000 to the power bills of this factory: "A hit on their bottom line, a potential hit on jobs." Standing to one side watching the politicians and the journalists and the cameras is one of the factory's owners, John Kernahan, who tells me Sulo's annual turnover is $85 million. So the carbon tax? "It's not a biggie."

The polls will soon suggest the same. Before the carbon tax began half of us thought we would be left worse off. A month later that number had fallen by 13 per cent. In that brief time, half the nation also came to the conclusion the tax wasn't going to make much difference to them at all. The *Australian Financial Review* reported both major parties were finding "voters are highly sceptical that the tax will ever be dumped." Abbott's blood pledge to set about repealing it on day one seems not to be believed. The carbon-tax scare campaign that has brought Abbott all this way may be running out of steam. In these early weeks of the tax, Labor's primary vote lifted a little.

The new minister would stand in his office every day before Question Time rehearsing answers to questions that rarely came his way. "My department used to love it," a senior bureaucrat told me. "They made the hard questions harder and harder and tried to catch him out. It became a kind of game which they thoroughly enjoyed." Abbott gave these rehearsals his all, mastering the detail, practising his rhetoric, gestures and quips. He was determined to shine in parliament, determined to meet any challenges that might come his way. He wanted no balls-ups by himself or his department. He wanted to be on top of any major issues that might arise. But his first priority was his own political performance. "He wanted the assurance from the department that nothing was going wrong underneath. But as long as that was the case, he didn't really want to get into all the detail of how the Job Network was actually running. He was not hands-on. He was generally interested in employment but he was not one of those ministers who run their department."

Abbott's task was to sort out the problems of a signature Howard initiative: putting the work of the old Commonwealth Employment Service out to tender. First he had to clear his own patch by confronting his senior minister, Peter Reith. In *Battlelines* he wrote:

> On my first day as his junior minister, it was Peter Reith, not me, who chaired an officials' meeting addressing a funding crisis in the Job Network, even though it was my immediate responsibility. The next morning I fronted my ministerial boss to say that I had no intention of remaining a glorified errand boy.

Reith pulled back. Abbott was a problem-solver, a talker, a charmer. He mastered what needed to be mastered. He had the money to fix the problems. Though he went about the task with a will, he clearly did not share the ideological conviction that the jobless were better off without help from the public service. Abbott's default position is that governments are there to act, to solve problems, not to withdraw and leave things to the cut and thrust of market forces. He was clearly not one of those conservatives who loved the market. His loyalty was to government and what government could achieve through intervention.

Abbott was a minister on the way up. Bureaucrats like working for them: they have more clout. Within a couple of years he would take over from Reith and enter cabinet; then in 2003 Howard would promote him to the behemoth portfolio of Health and Ageing, which he held until the government's fall. He began running a budget of a few hundred million and ended up with one of $30 billion a year. He began as a minor player and was quickly one of the best-known – at times notorious – ministers in the government. From beginning to end there were controversies. But there were no great catastrophes, no personal scandals. His ministerial career was packed into a decade: Abbott was still forty when it began and just fifty when it ended.

Bureaucrats put him among the better ministers, though with frustrating peculiarities. His handwriting is appalling. Even his numbers are illegible. Someone on his personal staff had to tell public servants what was actually scrawled on their submissions. He was reasonably efficient at turning paper around but not exceptional like Howard, who dealt with everything in forty-eight hours. They dreaded Easter when the minister disappeared on Pollie Pedal and would need to be tracked down in a crisis in some caravan park out in the boondocks. Everyone got in his ear on these rides. He wasn't bad at sifting out the rubbish but he did bring back some odd ideas to his departments. "As with all ministers," one bureaucrat remarked, "anecdote is very powerful." He was admirably polite and kept his temper, but staff dealings with him remained formal. He was rather buttoned-up. You got to know little about him. His public servants found it strange that he did so much writing. To their intense frustration Abbott would disappear for days behind closed doors to write another 900-word opinion piece for the *Australian*. He thought of himself as thoughtful, even intellectual, and loved playing with big ideas in this way.

But they tended not to be about the task at hand. There his contributions were useful rather than original. For the most part he left policy thinking to his departments. He and his office were not a source of fresh ideas. Bureaucrats found his staff intensely loyal and happy but relatively weak. Abbott's experience with Oldfield had cast a shadow, leaving him reluctant to hire figures of independent standing to work closely with him. A better office might have made Abbott a better minister. Clearly he was not excited by the business of public administration. That had to be done well but it was the responsibility of others. In his decade in the ministry, Abbott was engaged most intensely by the political process and the possibilities of gung-ho government action.

By late 1999 a third of the work once done by the CES had gone by tender to Christian agencies. Though the work was secular and the money – about $700 million a year – was public, some church agencies were demanding the right to hire only committed Christians to carry out their greatly expanded responsibilities. Buddhist community leaders protested. Jewish leaders went straight to the prime minister. As the controversy rolled on, there was no stauncher advocate for the prerogatives of Christianity than the minister. He argued that finding jobs was faith in action:

> It takes considerable resources of stamina and resilience to work with the long-term unemployed. The source of this commitment is of no concern to government. It could be an ideal of community service or professional pride as much as any religious belief in the brotherhood of man. What matters is that people working with job-seekers keep faith in themselves and in those they serve.

The Human Rights and Equal Opportunities Commission was equally certain that this was secular work being carried out with public money and should be performed according to secular rules blind to faith and sex. HREOC's draft guidelines were slammed by Abbott as "perilously close to discriminating against religion" and he railed against the depiction of himself in the press as a Catholic committed to protecting the privileges of his church. His rejoinder was lofty: "Any suggestion that practice of religion inherently devalues people's political judgments would be an ugly development in Australian public life."

But the criticism was fair. Abbott was protecting one of the most jealously guarded privileges of all churches, but particularly the Catholic Church: the right to employ in schools, hospitals and nursing homes only those who live according to the sex rules of the faith. Abbott put it this way:

> Organisations should not have to employ people who cannot support their fundamental principles. Expecting a church-based Job Network member to employ a gay activist, for instance, is as unreasonable as demanding that a Labor MP employ a leading member of the Liberal Party in his electorate office.

That's still the official church line: as enemies of the faith, homosexuals can properly be banned from teaching or sweeping the paths in a hospital yard or finding jobs for the long-term unemployed. Few countries in the world extend this privilege to religion. Though Abbott had to accept the agencies could employ "sympathetic" non-Christians, he fought off all attempts to challenge the core privilege of the churches to refuse to hire homosexuals – or adulterers, single mothers, transsexuals or any sinners of the bedroom. In the year it took to resolve this controversy, Abbott made his name in politics. He entered the public imagination as a Catholic warrior.

Homosexuality still baffles him. He has long abandoned the mission against dykes and poofters he pursued at university. But he still finds it odd that a footballer from a good Catholic family could turn out to be gay. He has homosexual friends. Some of them adore him. Michael Kirby worked with him at Australians for Constitutional Monarchy and thought him attractive, intelligent, articulate and down-to-earth. When Abbott's old school invited the High Court judge to address the senior boys, he chose homophobia as his theme. The day before the talk, Cardinal Clancy attacked the Gay and Lesbian Mardi Gras. The Anglican archbishop backed him. Both demanded homosexuals live celibate lives. Kirby's theme was: "It's okay if you're gay." The impact was exactly as he wished: thoughtful questioning at the school and big press coverage afterwards. Kirby's biographer A.J. Brown reports:

> Tony Abbott wrote to Kirby that he had trouble with the idea that homosexuality should be regarded as acceptable, rather than simply accepted: "especially when the overwhelming weight of tradition holds that it is in some sense sinful."

He can't let it go. A couple of years ago he caused a stir by telling Liz Hayes on 60 Minutes that he felt "a bit threatened" by homosexuality. He backtracked swiftly, as he so often does, from his more arresting statements, but on ABC Lateline a few nights later he was still arguing that homosexuality "challenges orthodox notions of the right order of things." These days he is as likely to say that homosexuals are merely different. But Abbott the true believer will not challenge his church. Not here and not, it seems, anywhere. He does not like the language but does not dissent from Vatican teaching on homosexuality. That his sister Christine Forster is lesbian has not shaken his faith. Politics Abbott talks difference but Values Abbott believes, as he always has, that homosexuality is, in the words of the church, an "intrinsic moral evil."

Abbott was under riding instructions from Howard not to talk outside his own portfolio. It wasn't easy. It curtailed the range of the opinion pieces he was churning out for the press, essentially vigorous polemics on the virtues of the Howard government. But on the great issue of these years, the monarchy versus the republic, everyone was free to speak and campaign. Support for getting rid of the Queen was at 57 per cent but the nation was divided on the kind of republic that should replace her, a division that proved the death of the proposal. This was minority politics – the power of the passionate minority to hold the line – played at a level of genius by Howard and with inexhaustible passion by his lieutenant

Tony Abbott. The republicans have never recovered. Abbott can claim a good measure of credit not only for wrecking the republican hopes in the 1999 referendum, but also for keeping them off the agenda ever since.

The victory came at a price. Words are weapons, says Abbott, and ever since his university days he has shown how powerfully he can deploy scorn and insult. He denounced a proposal to remove non-citizen British from the electoral rolls as "ethnic cleansing" as bodies were still being dug up in the former Yugoslavia. He declared one or other of the Costello brothers – Peter the treasurer and Tim the Baptist minister – was "telling whoppers," an insult that ended the old friendship between Abbott and the deputy leader of his party. He accused republicans in his own party of conducting a "proxy war" against Howard. He threw into the mix Churchill, Pétain, Charles de Gaulle, the failings of the Weimar republic and the rise of Hitler. In the *Sydney Morning Herald* at that time I set him some homework:

> Clearly explain how an Australian head of state with powers as proposed in the referendum could bring to office in Canberra a local equivalent of the most vicious dictator of the century?

He never justified the Hitler slur to anyone. His talent for personal abuse seemed depthless. Even friends in the press were reproaching him for going over the top. The prime minister began muzzling him. On a sour note for the monarchists, the republicans romped home in most of the rich and leafy suburbs of the nation, including the harbourside suburbs of Warringah.

After this victory Abbott was seen as a man to be reckoned with, a politician with a future. The press was interested. The first big newspaper and television profiles of him appeared. His story became known: university politician, boxer, would-be priest, monarchist, hard man of the right, the first minister to be ejected from the House in nearly forty years. He was clearly a protected species, spoken of as the prime minister's protégé, a rival to Costello and perhaps a contender for the highest office one day. Even so, a single question was being asked more than ever after the referendum campaign: did Abbott know where to draw the line?

After Howard's third big win in 2001, Abbott hoped for promotion, though he had been in Reith's old job as Minister for Employment, Workplace Relations and Small Business for less than a year. Instead, Howard put the young minister's aggression to use by also appointing him Leader of the House, a position he would hold until the fall of the government. The hard calls of parliamentary strategy plus the tough line on the unemployed being pursued by the Howard government made it easier than ever to portray Abbott as utterly hard-hearted. He famously denounced "job snobs" and freely quoted Christ's remarks about the poor being with us always. He had a number of controversial but not untruthful things to say about the causes of poverty:

> We can't stop people drinking, we can't stop people gambling, we can't stop people having substance problems, we can't stop people from making mistakes ...

Under Abbott, the unemployed had never had to work so hard to keep the dole. While he was pilloried for enforcing a severe regime of punishment to force them to look for jobs, he was trying behind the scenes to persuade the government to take another course entirely. He wanted tax breaks for those on welfare to encourage them to take work. This was his one big idea in the portfolio and he has cited it since as evidence that somewhere inside the Liberal Party the DLP was alive and well. But not very alive: the plan was killed off by Howard.

Abbott knew he had to counter the caricature of the Catholic hard man if his leadership ambitions were ever to go anywhere. He began to give extraordinary, wide-ranging interviews which earned him something of a reputation as a thinker. No Australian politician in living memory had spoken quite like this. Politics Abbott was muffled by his place in cabinet, but Values Abbott had free rein. A 2003 interview with Paul Kelly of the *Australian* was the template for the pieces that followed. As they drove for hours through the bush one day, Abbott told Kelly he saw politics as a way of giving glory to God:

> This idea that politics is a managerial exercise, a simple question of resource allocation, I just think is dead wrong because politics is about inspiring people and persuading people there is value in what they do.

That day with Kelly he returned to his signature worry: the cohesion of the world. In his maiden speech Abbott had said governments must be an "instrument for giving cohesion and purpose to our national life." A decade later he told Kelly national survival was at stake:

> Every Australian needs to feel some kind of mystical bond and union with every other Australian. If that is ever lost, if it is just a sort of collective self-interest as tenants in the same building, that's not enough for a nation to survive.

Santamaria used to talk like that: another divisive man with a mission to hold society together. Abbott doesn't have the same sense that we stand forever on the lip of doom. But like Santamaria he sees the fragility of society as a bedrock argument against change, particularly change welcomed by most but passionately opposed by few. Cultivating the fears and harnessing the rage of minorities is a great conservative skill. Abbott has it in spades. His pitch to the fearful is the nameless dread of change in a fragile world. And the rest of us are urged to leave well alone or the fearful will tear politics apart. It is a profoundly conservative brand of politics that deals in panic and threat. Keating says: "You know what Tony Abbott's policy is: 'If you don't give me the job, I'll wreck the place.'"

In his big-picture moods, Abbott's mind turns to the fate of Western civilisation. This is a vast grab-bag of everything he loves about the past and present: Christ, the Bible, Shakespeare, cricket, the welfare state – "an essential part of modern Western civilisation" – Winston Churchill and Edmund Burke. The list has grown over time to include "scientific and cultural curiosity, belief in the equality of man, freedom under the law, and a sense that diversity is a potential source of strength, not weakness." Western civilisation has Christian origins, a British bias and flourishes in the Anglosphere but its values are universal. "We don't support them because they're ours," Abbott says, "but because we think they are capable of being adopted by anyone, any place, anytime."

The Pope and the Queen represent "the oldest continuing institutions in Western civilisation." Other great defenders are Churchill, Santamaria and a number of obscure figures on the far right of Australian politics, including David Flint, the daffy gay lawyer who campaigned with Abbott against the republic. Abbott appears to count no one of the left among civilisation's defenders. Nor, despite his admiration for the United States, does Abbott count the Bill of Rights among the achievements of Western civilisation. Freedom and rights are oddly disconnected in his analysis. All the American wars from Vietnam to today were fought for civilisation's sake. The Coalition of the Willing went to war in Iraq "to uphold universal values … if it's possible to engage in an altruistic war, this was it."

Without hesitation Abbott declares "the whole edifice of Western civilisation" to rest on the church. Some might say the church had to be fought tooth and nail to allow liberal democracy to emerge, but Abbott claims we have the church to thank for "the presumption of innocence, universal suffrage, limited government, and religious, cultural and political pluralism." But deeper than that is Catholic teaching on birth, life and death, which he sees as "fundamental to the ethical underpinnings of Western civilisation." In a vast essay on the man and the papacy at the time of Benedict XVI's visit to Australia for World Youth Day, Abbott put his own worries about the fragility of all of this into the pontiff's mind: "The question haunting Benedict is whether our civilisation can maintain these principles while rejecting the religious insights on which they rest."

Such grand considerations hardly mattered for Abbott in public life until Howard unexpectedly promoted him to the portfolio of Health and Ageing in October 2003. Again there was a complex problem to be solved.

Doctors were threatening to abandon the public health system in the face of the looming failure of medical indemnity funds. Again Howard gave Abbott all the money he needed. He worked on the problems with the assistant treasurer, Helen Coonan: "He showed a great capacity to engage with people on various different levels: first of all the doctors, then insurance people at a fairly complex professional level – medical indemnity insurance and long tail insurance are pretty complex products – and he was quite able to empathise with patients. He managed to get everybody settled down on a temporary basis while we worked our way through it. We got a solution at last."

The medical profession liked dealing with Abbott. For the most part they found him sharp and refreshing. That he could muster so much money to address their worries naturally delighted them. After addressing the medical indemnity crisis, Abbott turned his attention very successfully to arresting the decline in bulk billing. But there were medicos who found their dealings with the minister puzzling. Adele Horin reported in the *Sydney Morning Herald*:

> Ian Hickie, professor of psychiatry, and executive director of the Brain and Mind Institute at the University of Sydney, stood in Abbott's Canberra office arguing the case for more federal money for mental health. Abbott, then minister for health, was his customary engaging self. And Hickie soon found himself in a philosophical discussion about the nature of mental illness. "Abbott believed people should be able to control their thoughts and emotions; he believed they should exercise free will," Hickie says. "He admitted his own views made it hard for him to understand mental health issues."

Out of this exchange and an intervention by Howard came a $1.5 billion commitment to the first national mental health plan. A happy Hickie verdict on Abbott: "He's not a reformer; he's a great opportunist."

Abbott had moved from a portfolio where the Commonwealth ran the show to one where control of his vast responsibilities was shared with the states. He found this frustrating. He couldn't simply intervene. He had to work through others. He hated the muddle of federal structures. He liked to be able to make clean, final decisions. Officers in his department wondered if the minister was closing his door to write all those opinion pieces because they had the clarity his work now lacked. He could put his position without having to deal with the constitutional limits of Commonwealth authority or the difficulties of manoeuvring it through the COAG process.

Abbott's one big idea in Health was for the Commonwealth to take control of all the nation's hospitals. This required a shift in his thinking. In the Keating years he had declared that Australia had "a perfectly good system of government provided each tier minds its own business." He didn't think so any longer. "As a new backbencher, I had not anticipated how hard this was, given that voters don't care who solves their problems, they just want them solved." As Minister for Health he lit on a new guiding conservative principle: "Power divided is power controlled." He had in mind an enormous reform that would reshape Canberra's relations with the states. He was roundly mocked in cabinet. His senior bureaucrats put a lot of work into talking him down. Did he really want to be responsible for every asthma patient who had to wait too long in an emergency department? Eventually he was persuaded that Commonwealth public servants could not run hospitals any better than state public servants. This was the argument that got him, but he found it frustrating.

The health department was enormous. It had a budget as big as that of New South Wales. There were junior ministers, parliamentary secretaries and a team of deputy heads. Every parliamentary session Abbott brought them all together to discuss the issues that might emerge over the weeks to come. Such openness was unprecedented, kept everyone up to date and diffused the tensions that usually plague the parliamentary team serving a big portfolio. He was a good chair. He continued to hold a half-hour prep session before each Question Time. Now there was no lack of questions. Those working with the new minister were surprised by the contrast between his performances in the department and in parliament.

Among the bureaucrats he was patient, polite and listened to – but did not enjoy – criticism. There are ministers who relish slashing budgets, wielding the knife with macho pleasure. Abbott wasn't one of them. "He wasn't ruthless," said an observer of his time in the portfolio. "He didn't have an appetite for nasties. Cuts were never explored with relish. People find this amazing but he doesn't seek conflict."

Howard went to the 2004 elections having made cast-iron promises to keep Medicare's generous safety-net provisions. But after unexpectedly winning control of the Senate, Howard and Costello decided to renege. Abbott was distressed. He left Howard to announce the decision and withdrew to consider his future in the face of furious ridicule over this broken promise. "If we hadn't controlled the Senate, I would never have had to eat that particular shit sandwich," Abbott told Peter Hartcher. "Getting control of the Senate was a curse. It allowed us to do things that we would not normally have been able to get away with and I think it tempted us to chance our arm in ways which ultimately did us significant political damage." In the end, he decided to stay in cabinet. He didn't bitch and moan to the press gallery. He went back to work.

One day he was asked how he, a Catholic, could preside over a system that funded 80,000 abortions a year. This was soon after he took over the Health portfolio and he brooded over the answer for five months. Then, at a rowdy meeting of the Adelaide University Democratic Club, he reignited a debate no federal politician had touched for twenty-five years:

> The problem with the Australian practice of abortion is that an objectively grave matter has been reduced to a question of the mother's convenience. Aborting a first trimester foetus is not morally identical to deliberately killing a living human being, but it's not just removing a wart or a cyst either. Even those who think that abortion is a woman's right should be troubled by the fact that 100,000 Australian women choose to destroy their unborn babies every year.

Abbott was being deliberately provocative and belittling. His was the language not of a politician, but a Vatican ideologue. He condemned women for taking the "easy way out" and declared abortion a national tragedy. He complained his constituents were more concerned with boat people than foetuses. It must have seemed to him like the old days of campus politics, when protesters were dragged from the meeting shouting, "Get your rosaries off our ovaries."

Abbott is still living with the repercussions of that speech. Women recoiled from him. Peter Costello went on air immediately to hose down fears that Medicare funding for abortions was about to end. In public Howard supported Abbott's right to raise the issue but was reported to be appalled in private. The Minister for Health seemed to have done his prospects in the Coalition great harm. "He's just too right-wing," Dennis Atkins reported a Costello backer saying. "You can't hold passionate anti-abortion views and lead a mainstream party, let alone lead the nation." The women of parliament organised to end his ministerial veto on the importation of the morning-after pill RU486. He was deeply hurt by this. He saw hypocrisy and scare-mongering all around him as the hullabaloo continued month after month. He stuck to his defence that he had spoken as a Christian but had *done* nothing about abortion as Minister for Health.

So why stir up this hornets' nest? The answer lies deep in his faith. Abbott feels obliged as a Christian to keep a lost political cause alive. Abbott the politician knows he can't roll back the law on abortion, but Abbott the rock-solid Catholic is not going to abandon the possibility. He cannot reassure the women of Australia that he will never try. In Abbott's book, Christian politicians are obliged to keep the faith and do as much as they can when they can. Unless it's a matter of the most extraordinary moment and a point of honour, there's no sense asking the public to do what it simply won't do. But the believer in office must always try to move the debate in the right direction. And they must be willing to wait. Those who wonder at the patience of figures like Abbott forget they have eternity in their heads.

Howard stepped in to shut the abortion debate down. A few weeks later, Daniel O'Connor, a 27-year-old television cameraman, contacted his birth mother for the first time. She was Abbott's university girlfriend, now Kathy Donnelly. What followed was excruciating for everyone and beautifully handled by Abbott. It is perhaps the only time in his career that the nation's heart went out to him. He was on his way to mass on Boxing Day, 2004, when a message came from Donnelly. After mass and a talk with Margie he rang. He met O'Connor. He thought the young man looked a little like his eldest daughter. The world was let in on the soap opera via a nine-page spread in the *Bulletin* with moody photographs and a contribution from Abbott that ended: "Margie and my daughters have accepted Daniel as a family member. For me, this is important, a new start, a second chance." The mother's university flatmate looked at the *Bulletin* pictures. The resemblance was so strong. DNA samples were provided. Three weeks after the news broke, it was all over: O'Connor was not the long-lost son Abbott had imagined for so long was out there. "I'm sorry," he said, "that poor old Daniel has been dragged through the public spotlight as a result of a connection to me, which it now appears was never the case."

From the moment he entered cabinet, Abbott took more seriously than many of his colleagues the notion of discussing the nation's affairs around the table. "He was quite inclined to second-guess most things," says Helen Coonan. "Right at the end of a discussion he might say: 'A thought, can I offer a thought, Prime Minister?' And his thoughts were not bad ones. He's somebody who's capable of thinking outside the square. He used to be able to see other dimensions to problems. I think he irritated a lot of people who might not have taken too kindly to it. But I think he made a very useful contribution. And it's very Jesuitical, of course. I think he was true to his upbringing, his roots, his value system." He attended closely to deliberations that ranged far outside his own portfolios. At that point, ministers often discreetly work on their own papers. But Abbott liked to listen. He didn't come to cabinet with his mind made up about everything. He thought things through in the room. It was an unusual quality. That Howard allowed him such a long rein used to exasperate his colleagues, often the same ones who despaired of his stream of suggestions for Canberra's intervention. Costello wrote:

> Never one to be held back by the financial consequences of decisions, he had grandiose plans for public expenditure. At one point when we were in government, he asked for funding to pay for telephone and electricity wires to be put underground throughout the whole of his northern Sydney electorate to improve the amenity of the neighbourhoods. He also wanted the Commonwealth to take over the building of local roads and bridges in his electorate. He wanted the Commonwealth to take over hospitals. He used to tell me proudly that he had learned all of his economics at the feet of Bob Santamaria. I was horrified.

Costello and the hard right's Nick Minchin used to tease him as he proposed they intervene here or give money there. The tone was good-humoured. The verdict wasn't: "There he goes, channelling Bob again."

He certainly was when it came to the unfinished business of breaking student unions. As the boisterous president of the SRC young Tony had begged the Fraser government without success to intervene. Now three key figures in that old campaign – Abbott, Costello and the Special Minister of State Eric Abetz – were perfectly placed to pursue their old vendetta against left-wing student politics. A first bill for the abolition of compulsory student union fees failed in 2004 but it was back as soon as the government won control of the Senate. Old passions were rekindled on both sides. Such were police fears that in August 2005 Abbott was warned not to debate Julia Gillard in the Manning Bar at Sydney University. This was huge news. Abbott berated the police: "You have given a victory to the enemies of a free society." But the bill was also loathed by the National Party because it would drain university sporting clubs of cash. Out in the bush, those clubs and that money mattered. The bill

passed by only one vote. Barnaby Joyce crossed the floor. Abbott had realised an old ambition but now the Nationals reckoned they were owed a
favour.

Control of the Senate also let Howard pursue ambitions going back to
the earliest days of his own politics: he would break the unions. This was
not in Abbott's DNA. He thought WorkChoices harsh and bad politics: "A
catastrophic political blunder because it undermined the Howard battlers'
faith in the Prime Minister's goodwill." He and another Catholic warrior
in the government, Kevin Andrews, contested the proposals in cabinet.
They did not advance the underlying moral arguments but questioned
how the politics would play out and whether WorkChoices would be seen
to be going too far. Abbott was particularly concerned with the abolition
of the no-disadvantage test, which had set a safety net under earlier workplace reform. He told cabinet: "It was always going to look as though we
were exposing vulnerable people to danger." Howard had his way.

Not for the first time, Abbott was left to defend a policy he deplored
and his church opposed. Indeed, there was an ecumenical wall of opposition. Abbott knew WorkChoices was pretty damaging among broadly
Catholic circles because they felt that it was contrary to that strain of
social justice that they had taken very much to heart. He had been through
this before. Abbott is familiar with the argument that Hewson lost in
1993 when the Catholic vote deserted the Coalition over *Fightback!* He
knew how close Howard came to defeat in 1998 when the churches again
came out against the GST. He knew how lucky the government was when
George Pell, then the Archbishop of Melbourne, broke ranks with his fellow bishops to declare: "There is no one Catholic position on an issue as
complex as taxation." Howard had seized on that as a lifeline. Abbott had
also, in his time, suffered Christian opposition to his government's
approach to native title, refugees and waterfront reform.

Being taken to task by clerics infuriates him. He takes their attacks
personally and his rhetoric in reply is particularly insulting. It is easier for
him when he disagrees with his clerical accusers. He simply denounces

them as partisan lefties, accuses them of "moral snobbery" and claims they are just crawling to their congregations:

> Finding fault with government is always more popular than telling parishioners to lift their game or confronting the church's own failings and has probably become the clerical equivalent of kicking the dog on the way home from a bad day at the office.

But it is tougher when Politics Abbott finds himself in conflict with Values Abbott. He and his critics saw eye to eye on WorkChoices. He had signed up to the social teachings of the church as a child. It was integral to the mission Santamaria sent him into the world to pursue. Abbott had never reneged on them. He believed they embodied values that helped hold society together. So when the crunch came over WorkChoices, where did his loyalties lie?

Politics won. As the government slid towards oblivion, Abbott's only loyalty was to Howard. It was an impeccably secular response. He put aside his own values. He respected cabinet solidarity. He did not, despite reports at the time, tell the clerics to butt out of political debate. He took them on. His language was memorably appalling as he demanded they get off the government's back:

> A political argument is not transformed into a moral argument simply because it's delivered with an enormous dollop of sanctimony. I do think that if churchmen spent more time encouraging virtue in people and less time demanding virtue from governments we would have ultimately a better society.

WorkChoices was killing Howard by early 2007. So was Kyoto. Howard had turned his back on the treaty as an act of solidarity with George W. Bush. But with the country locked in drought, Australians were demanding action. A few days after Labor installed its new leader, Kevin Rudd, the prime minister set up a committee of industrialists and bureaucrats which backed the notion of an emissions trading system. But there seemed little or no hope that a deeply divided cabinet would sign up to the idea. The ultimate sceptic Nick Minchin led the hostile right and Malcolm Turnbull the enthusiastic left. Abbott was a swinging voter. He kept his mind open for a long time. He thought it through in cabinet. His support, when it came, was driven not by science but politics. Abbott's thinking, according to a close observer, was this: "There is a mood in the country: the bloody farmers think this drought is to do with climate change; we've got all these green initiatives but nobody thinks we're doing anything; we're going to meet our Kyoto targets yet we don't ratify. I think this is the time to go forward." Abbott helped Howard over the line. On 1 June 2007 the prime minister announced a cap and trade system, with targets to be set sometime after the election.

Abbott now faced a more agonising choice. Howard had been a father to him in politics for twenty years. He owed every step on the ladder – from his first job in John Hewson's office to the mighty portfolio of Health – to Howard's patronage. He had, like an impatient son, opposed him at times, but he had always been forgiven and favoured. Tony was Howard's golden boy. Everyone in cabinet knew this. He had absorbed most of the old man's politics so long ago he might have been born with them. Sitting with him in cabinet had been a masterclass in leadership. *Battlelines* is a drab book on the whole but there are passages like this that sing:

> Political leadership is not like running a company or being captain of a ship. Prime ministers can direct public servants, but, for all their prominence and influence, they can rarely give orders to their colleagues. Howard understood that respect had to be earned, affection had to be won, and authority had to be used sparingly if it was to be effective ... Howard's ability to be a successful prime minister for almost twelve years is the supreme personal achievement of modern Australian politics.

But by the winter of 2007, Howard's political capital was exhausted. The infinitely gutless Costello was standing by as Alexander Downer began sounding out their cabinet colleagues on the margins of APEC. "We were in parallel universes," Costello wrote. "Face-to-face meetings with world leaders and meetings at night to canvass Howard's departure." Abbott faltered. On the afternoon of Wednesday 5 September, he had conversations with Costello and Downer that led both to believe he wanted Howard to step down. "Abbott thought a change might give us a chance to win," Costello wrote. But that evening, after more phone calls, Abbott rang Kirribilli House to pledge his undying support. Abbott would tell Liz Jackson of Four Corners: "From the very beginning of the government to its last day, I thought John Howard was the best man to lead the team."

He had a bad election campaign. He stumbled and told the truth one night: workers had lost protections under WorkChoices. He lingered too long with Howard in Melbourne one day and was thirty-five minutes late for a debate with the shadow minister for Health, Nicola Roxon, at the National Press Club. They had a tight-lipped exchange as they shook hands for the cameras:

> Roxon: "You can't even get here on time, it must be a battle."
> Abbott: "It certainly wasn't intentional."
> Roxon: "You can control these things, mate. I'm sure had you wanted to, you could."
> Abbott: "That's bullshit. You're being deliberately unpleasant. I suppose you can't help yourself, can you?"

The microphones picked up the word "bullshit" loud and clear. It might not have done him so much damage were he not that day also under attack for abusing Bernie Banton. The dying anti-asbestos campaigner had turned up in a wheelchair outside Abbott's electoral office in Manly to mount a little protest over the government's reluctance to subsidise a new and expensive drug to treat mesothelioma, the condition killing him. Abbott took an ugly swipe at Banton. "Look, it was a stunt," he told Channel Nine. "Let's be upfront about this. I know Bernie is very sick but just because a person is sick doesn't mean that he is necessarily pure of heart in all things." In his trademark way Abbott was using the language of faith as an insult. He was left apologising all the way to election day.

At about 10 p.m. on 24 November Howard rang Rudd. He had lost government and his seat. A few minutes after conceding defeat he addressed the nation. He thanked the people of Australia and wished the new government "the very best of good fortune in the years ahead." Abbott's political world collapsed around him. He had kept his seat but lost his patron. Also gone was his ministerial salary. His colleagues were furious about his campaign blunders. Why was it that Tony never knew when to hold his tongue, where to draw the line? Where was his judgment? Where was his heart?

Bronwyn Bishop gets the biggest cheer of all from the party workers assembled in the big dark room on the fourth floor of the leagues club. What an old stager: the hair, the heels, the fox around the neck, the raw enthusiasm for the limelight and the fight. They take her to their hearts like a club act remembered fondly from a long time ago. On this Sunday afternoon in the western suburbs of Sydney, Tony Abbott is introducing his candidates to the men and women who will hand out the leaflets, staff the booths and scrutinise the count for the Liberal Party. The applause tells us better than any polling can what's hitting the spot with the party faithful.

"We are in this position today we could not have dreamed of because of Tony Abbott," declares the warm-up act, Arthur Sinodinos. "He is working his guts out, laser-focused." Applause erupts. These people don't share the doubts and hesitations of so much of Australia. Their eyes are bright. Abbott turns them on. Sinodinos is washed with applause as he lays it on thicker and thicker. Abbott is an action man in the best sense of the word; he is not afraid to stand against the tide; he loves campaigning in factories against the carbon tax; he's not the sort of man who would out his sister as a lesbian on Q&A. "He is a flesh-and-blood human being. He's not Mother Teresa in drag."

Abbott provokes such decibels of applause only once but it is a telling moment. He's speaking in front of four neatly furled Australian flags. Around the hall hang banners showing Indonesian fishing boats and the words SECURE OUR BORDERS. We've already heard the campaign anthem sung in a drawl that's part Tamworth and part Tennessee: "That's our Australia, let's make it strong." And up on stage – dressed not in the blue and white habit of the Missionaries of Charity but his Liberal Party uniform of grey suit, white shirt and blue tie – Abbott sends the applause off the dial with this: "The fact is, John Howard stopped the boats."

His stump speech is good. Very good. The words are plain, the images are sharp, the rhetoric discreetly Churchillian as he introduces the candidates:

> You will see them at your bus stops, you will see them at your railway stations, you will see them in your shopping centres, you will see them knocking on your doors ... They will be visible, because Labor is in hiding. Labor is in hiding from the people of Western Sydney. Labor is particularly in hiding from the businesses of Western Sydney, because what Labor has given the businesses and the job providers of Western Sydney is nothing but pain.

Political leaders need a name for their flock. It's a crucial branding exercise, shorthand for both the politics and the politician. Menzies had his "forgotten people," Keating his "working families" and John Howard his unique "battlers." Abbott came up with a twist on Menzies in May last year, the clunky but heartfelt "forgotten families." He's pitching to them again in Parramatta:

> I often talk about the forgotten families of Australia, but no families anywhere in this country have been more forgotten than the families of Western Sydney. You have been denied infrastructure, you have been denied attention by a political movement that for too long has taken you for granted. Well, I will never take you for granted. None of my candidates will ever take you for granted.

Family has its own meaning for Abbott. He believes families hold the world together. His sort of families are, of course, heterosexual. He won't have men marrying each other. Ditto women. Nor does he want gay and lesbian couples to bring up children. He strongly disapproves of them being allowed to adopt and of lesbians having access to IVF. He is rigidly hard-line Catholic on all this. He doesn't quite say it would be better if such children were never adopted or never born but he birches the parents for their thoughtless indulgence: "Only the most starry-eyed member of the Woodstock generation would maintain that a parent's self-fulfil-ment readily justifies depriving children of living with both a mother and a father, especially when the children are young."

Like everyone on earth he would prefer marriages to last. But in *Battle-lines* he sketched a plan to bring back fault-based divorce – adultery, cru-elty, private detectives etc. – for those who opt for what they call in America a covenant marriage, which Abbott sees as "a type of marriage that approximates to the Christian ideal." The idea seems to have sunk like a stone. More durable has been the policy he sprang on his party soon after becoming leader: a $3.3 billion-a-year paid parental-leave scheme funded by business. For him and the Liberals it was totally left-field. Women who earn more will be paid more while on leave. Eventually, the payments will be taken over by the Commonwealth. After announcing the scheme, Abbott sought with some charm the absolution of his startled party. "Sometimes," he said, "it is better to ask forgiveness rather than permission."

Santamaria raged against working mothers. Abbott is married to one. She runs community-based child care. Abbott credits her with alerting him to the needs of children whose parents work, their care and early education. And he acknowledges with great candour that she, essentially, brought up their three daughters. The inevitable lot of a family-values politician is to spend a great deal of time away from the family. This cham-pion of self-reliance, the man who made the unemployed work for the dole, has no doubt that families like his deserve a great deal of help from the government. Twenty years ago he declared "middle-income families with children" to be "Australia's new poor." He doesn't see private health insurance rebates or support for private school education as middle-class welfare. He sees it as backing family aspiration, sound public policy encouraging people to do more for themselves. And help should not be cut off simply because a family is earning a hundred thousand dollars or more a year. It's in the Parramatta stump speech and earns an ovation:

you are people who want to do the right thing by yourselves and your families and you are not rich. Julia Gillard thinks you are rich. Julia Gillard thinks that a policeman married to a shop assistant is rich. Julia Gillard thinks that two schoolteachers bringing up a family together are rich. Well, I say you aren't rich. You are decent Australians wanting to get ahead and we will always stand by you.

Out by the escalators he gives a brief press conference under a sign offering 50 per cent off the club's live seafood banquet. His answers are perfunctory. Earlier that morning he was on *Insiders*. I was there, watching from the couch as he avoided Barrie Cassidy's questions. Abbott gave a boxer's performance: ducking, weaving and blocking. I found it dispiriting. Abbott must have too, for the transcript never makes it to his website. But those among the faithful at the leagues club who saw the show think he was terrific. Why? Because he gave nothing away. Abbott departs. His followers disperse into the winter afternoon. The background music in the foyer is Creedence Clearwater Revival's "Bad Moon Rising."

MR LUCKY

Abbott had dropped his daughters at the bus stop and was driving back across Roseville Bridge at about 7.30 a.m. when he turned on 2GB and heard Malcolm Turnbull having a set-to with Alan Jones. If you listen to a tape of that 2 November 2009 exchange now, you hear Turnbull refusing to kowtow to Jones, who becomes hysterically agitated about the "hoax" of global warming and a secret deal by world leaders which will bleed $50 billion from Australia and send it off to South America. Turnbull is sharp with Jones once or twice, asking to be heard, reminding him his heroes Margaret Thatcher and John Howard wanted action on global warming: "Don't you think," asks the leader of the Opposition, "you sound like the old lady who says the whole world is mad except for thee and me, and I have my doubts about thee?"

Abbott thought Turnbull's leadership was terminal at that moment. What he was hearing was a bar-room brawl between his leader and the guru of a great swathe of the Liberal Party. This was no way to deal with Alan Jones. Turnbull wasn't showing the necessary respect. It would cause immense damage.

Abbott was all over the shop on emissions trading. He feared destruction at the ballot box if the Opposition blocked Rudd. "The government's emissions trading scheme is the perfect political response to the public's fears," he had said in late July 2009. "It's a plausible means to limit carbon emissions that doesn't impose any obvious costs on voters." But behind the scenes he was already questioning the reality of global warming. In late September his tongue got the better of him at a meeting of farmers in Beaufort north of Melbourne. He said: "The argument on climate change is absolute crap." He backtracked afterwards as he always did, but that was the view of the man who now had his ear, the arch-denier Nick Minchin. They had a conversation next day as Abbott drove back from Beaufort that crystallised his thinking: the only way to avoid a catastrophic split inside the Coalition was to reject the ETS. But he was still wavering weeks later when he heard the exchange between Turnbull and Jones. Another three weeks passed before he finally told the party he had moved into the opponents' camp. This was his sixth position on the ETS. In *Shitstorm*, Lenore Taylor and David Uren wrote:

> his constant changes of heart were the subject of "ridicule" in shadow cabinet meetings. Abbott had a reputation as a "conviction" politician, but on this issue his position appeared to depend entirely on his reading of the polls and the mood of his party.

Coalition politicians were under intense pressure from the minerals and energy lobby. Tens of thousands of phone calls, emails and letters flooded their offices. Helen Coonan received 8000 emails calling on the Opposition to reject Rudd's ETS. Alan Jones was rampaging across the political landscape, broadcasting the wildest claims of the deniers. Abbott and Minchin were now leading a team of far-right figures on the Coalition back bench, many of them veterans of ACM's campaign against the republic. On 26 November the two men told Turnbull he must delay a vote on the ETS until after the looming Copenhagen conference or lose his job. Turnbull refused. Next day Abbott announced he was challenging. Four days later he was the leader of the Opposition.

Abbott had taken only two years to climb from humiliation to victory. After Howard's defeat he threw his hat in the ring. He didn't expect to win the leadership. He was doing what young politicians do to show they see themselves as contenders one day. His bid provoked mockery. Annabel Crabb latched onto his claim to have the "people skills" needed for the job. She has never let go. His colleagues had not forgotten Bernie Banton and they, unlike him, wished to put Howard behind them. Loyalty is deep in Abbott's DNA. He wouldn't betray his master. Again he drew the lesson that he must muffle his beliefs:

> this constant message that I got was: "You're too hard-line – you turn people off." So, lest anyone think that the art of success in democratic

politics is to have principles and to proclaim them very loudly; lest anyone think that in the words of Scripture we should "set ye up a standard in the land" and "blow the trumpet amongst the nations" (Jeremiah 51:27), we need to know that, if that is done, the result is just as likely to be defeat and failure, as triumphant success.

When he realised he had only five or six supporters in the party room, he withdrew from the race. Brendan Nelson became leader and demoted him to the junior post of shadow minister for Families, Community Services, Indigenous Affairs and the Voluntary Sector. Nelson said patronisingly: "This will be the making of him." Abbott was a bit player again. He withdrew to a tiny office in a far wing of parliament, hung a picture of the Queen on the wall and wondered what to do next. Only later did he realise what he was going through: bereavement.

Nelson lasted less than a year. These were scrappy months for Abbott. He remained withdrawn, at times not bothering to turn up to shadow cabinet. For days or weeks, colleagues didn't know where to find him. Opposition brought a $90,000-a-year pay cut and financial difficulties for a man who seems hardly to have a materialistic bone in his body. He needed another mortgage. His sister Christine Forster let him know she had left her husband for a woman. The apostle of Catholic family values found himself dealing with human reality very close to home. He coped. He was not entirely out of the public eye. Just as Kevin Rudd had used Seven's *Sunrise* to win himself a wider public, Abbott chose a new ABC television show, *Q&A*. He was the most frequent guest in its first couple of years. Early on he found himself on a panel with the publisher Louise Adler, who persuaded him to write the memoir cum manifesto that became *Battlelines*. Abbott hoped to pay off a chunk of the mortgage and work on softening his image. But such a book always has another purpose: it's a job application.

When Nelson fell in September 2008, Abbott supported Turnbull. A fortnight later the navy stopped a boat near the Ashmore islands carrying a dozen asylum seekers, mostly Afghans. It was only the second since Rudd had won office. There would be six more in 2008. The boats were back. For now the public was not particularly concerned. Rudd appeared untouchable.

Abbott wrote. As he worked on *Battlelines* he churned out dozens of opinion pieces. He was against sentimental attitudes to Aborigines; against Rudd's blather in parliament and twaddle in the *Monthly*; for paying maternity leave even to stay-at-home mothers; for George W. Bush giving John Howard the Congressional Medal of Freedom; for middle-class welfare to build a fair society; against guest workers coming in from the Pacific islands; for Michael Kirby on his retirement from the High Court; against the Rudd government's plans for halving rates of homelessness; for riding bicycles; for the NSW hard-right Christian faction leader David Clarke; against regarding the GFC as "a fundamental crisis in capitalism"; for Canberra being given all power in all fields in order that "the national government calls the shots"; and very much for the visit of "meek, shy, courtly, modest" Pope Benedict and 500 bishops for World Youth Day.

Turnbull shuffled his front bench in February 2009 and gave Abbott nothing new. Abbott would tell Tom Dusevic of the *Australian*:

> I was none too pleased, not to put too fine a point on it, about this reshuffle and I told Malcolm in the most extraordinarily blunt terms how disappointed and annoyed I was. He countered by telling me quite plainly that I'd been psychologically AWOL for much of the previous fifteen months, or whatever it was, and after I reflected on that I thought perhaps there was some point to what he said. And I thought, "Yeah, I do need to move on."

Abbott's luck had seemed to run out with the fall of Howard but in the winter of 2009 it began to run in his favour once again. Rudd and Turnbull both stumbled. The prime minister was so keen to exploit division in the Coalition over the ETS that he failed to clinch a deal with the Opposition. And Turnbull went off on one of the great wild-goose chases of

Australian politics. Godwin Grech, an Opposition source inside Treasury, persuaded him that Rudd's office had given special consideration to the Ipswich car dealer who lent the prime minister a 1996 Mazda Bravo ute to use in his electorate. Turnbull called for Rudd's resignation. But when the key email that was supposed to prove the prime minister's corruption finally saw the light of day, it turned out to be a fraud. Turnbull's reputation was shattered. Support for the Coalition nosedived. Nielsen put Labor ahead on a two-party-preferred basis 58 per cent to the Coalition's 42 per cent. An election would see the Opposition crushed.

Christopher Pyne was in Jerusalem the day the Coalition had to face the wreckage in parliament. Abbott took his place as manager of Opposition business and performed brilliantly: he placed his body in the line of fire; he rained down points of order; he threw Goebbels into the debate; he hounded Rudd over his links to the car dealer; and did what he could to present the wretched Grech as a heroic whistleblower and his leader as a parliamentary titan: "The Labor Party threw everything at Malcolm and he did not flinch." The party and the Canberra press gallery saw a resurgent Abbott. "After a year and a bit of what has at times looked dangerously like a sulk," wrote Annabel Crabb, "People Skills has got the lead back in his pencil."

Battlelines was launched a few weeks later. This odd, thin book was taken seriously by commentators and its author had a chance in the interviews that followed to be several of his many selves: Values Abbott, Politics Abbott and even Intellectual Abbott. It was big-picture time. *Battlelines* was clearly a calling card for national attention, a reminder to the people of Australia that there was another leader in waiting. He rather slavishly praised Turnbull as he nakedly promoted fresh directions for the party. Crippled by the Godwin Grech affair, Turnbull was losing his struggle to control the backwoodsmen, the sceptics and the friends of energy and minerals industries on the Opposition benches. As his troops began to mutiny, pollsters were searching for a new Liberal leader. They did not pick Abbott. He came last by a long way. Turnbull still had strong support.

But in the days before the 1 December challenge, the man most Australians wanted to lead the Liberal Party was Joe Hockey.

Abbott went into the party room with a few scribbled notes of an acceptance speech just in case he won. Until the last minute it had seemed only a remote possibility. Turnbull was supposed to be eliminated in the first round of voting. He wasn't. Hockey went instead. This was sheer luck, not design. The party was left to choose between a man who had come to exasperate them and a fresh contender who was willing to save them from the difficult challenge of emissions trading. One member of the party was absent, sick. Another scrawled "NO" on the ballot paper. Abbott won by a vote. He immediately called for a secret ballot to decide whether to block Rudd's ETS in the Senate. The procedure was impeccable and the result decisive: 54 votes to 29. The bipartisan alliance on global warming was over. A few days later, Rudd went off to the Copenhagen summit empty-handed.

Abbott's election would prove a big win for the forces of climate change denial in Australia. Campaigners once considered ratbags began to be taken seriously by the media. Fronts formed. Alliances were made. Many of the groups clamouring for Abbott's attention over the years that followed believe climate change is a hoax designed to create a world government run by a cabal of fabulously wealthy bankers. Alan Jones is patron of the Galileo Movement that argues just that. But the first fortune obviously in play was Gina Rinehart's, as she footed the bill for Viscount Monckton to campaign in Western Australia. Abbott positioned himself in this mayhem with enough wiggle room to put the science aside and only play the politics. The climate is not warming but changing, he says. Humans and greenhouse gases play a role, but only a role. These lines come straight from the handbooks of the denialists. Abbott is speaking their language.

Young Tony did well in science at Riverview. It's not a blind spot. But his real skill is politics. He hadn't betrayed his deepest self in shifting from support to opposition. What changed was his grasp of how the politics might be played. A mentor had come along to persuade him the world was in the grip of shallow and fashionable ideas. There was a mission here for a brave man to confront the zeitgeist. The Coalition was splintering. A hero was required. It was the republican referendum all over again. At this point the figures were against him: there was still a big majority for change but a passionate minority for blocking change. Abbott would bring to bear what had proved so magnificently effective before: fear, doubt, confusion and scorn. Naturally, he did not put the challenge he faced in quite those words. Three days after his victory he sat down and wrote a postscript for *Battlelines* that came to this rather colourful conclusion:

> When Winston Churchill drove to Buckingham Palace in the dark days of 1940 to accept the king's commission, he felt that his whole life had been but a preparation for this moment, or so he recounts in his memoirs. This is not wartime Britain. And I am certainly not Churchill. Still, I feel well equipped to take on the leadership of the party in what are testing times for the conservative side of politics.

SKIN IN THE GAME: HOUSE OF REPRESENTATIVES, 1 JUNE 2010

"PHO-NEY!" yell the government benches as Abbott comes to the dispatch box. "PHO-NEY! PHO-NEY!" The daily brawl is underway. To a wall of howls, groans and snatches of song, Rudd battles to say nothing new about Pink Batts. Two Liberals are thrown out. "On yer boat," yells Labor's Sid Sidebottom as the Opposition spokesman for punishing refugees, Scott Morrison, heads for the sin bin.

Each question is worse than the last. By number three – government hypocrisy over government advertising – the Opposition is baying for blood, an animal sound I haven't heard since playground brawls at Gordon Public a very long time ago. Bronwyn Bishop, doing what she can to bring chaos to the disorder, is silenced by the Speaker before she utters a word. Limp in her hands is a copy of Standing Orders bookmarked like an evangelist's Bible. Her mouth sags in disbelief.

Maybe there was an era when parliamentarians sat up straight and paid attention in the House. Not now. Even in the tumult of Question Time, half of them are slumped over one electronic device or another. Malcolm Turnbull is showing off his weekend purchase of a 64-gig, 3G-connected iPad. He is always at the cutting edge. The party's fallen leader is tapping the screen as if totting up a café bill. Two flat whites: tap. The pastrami baguette: tap. Sparkling mineral water: tap.

But Abbott is where it matters and where no one but he and his doting family ever expected to see him: down the front in the swivel chair, clear of the rabble behind him, facing the rabble in front. In six months, Abbott has made Rudd and his government look shabby. He's good at this. Baiting is his forte. He knows the cruel truth that the baiter is never blamed when victims lose their cool. His own mask never slips. He makes the government play his game in the House and they don't look like a government and Rudd doesn't look like a prime minister.

Abbott is only human. In government he complained about the Opposition taking too literally the advice of Lord Randolph Churchill: "Oppose everything, suggest nothing, and turf the government out." In opposition he has taken the advice to heart. Other models were available, particularly for a political leader who claims to worship at the shrine of Bob Menzies. His strategy was to oppose selectively and use opposition as a time for study and renewal. Menzies rejected advice urged on him during the war to attack the government daily in order to keep his name in the papers:

> It would seem quite picturesque for a few weeks, but before long the electors would begin to say, "Oh, here's Menzies again! He wants us to believe that the Government is *always* wrong." And they would soon weary of my attitude.

Abbott ditched Menzies in favour of Churchill Sr, John Howard and the strategists of the US Republican Party who discovered, a decade or so ago, that a campaign of absolute opposition can play havoc with an administration. Abbott couldn't quite follow the American recipe: he couldn't fire up the electorate on abortion or paint government itself as the enemy. But he could rail against debt — though we essentially have none — and he could pursue a strategy of continuous scorn. Josh Gordon of the *Sunday Age* saw the parallels early: "Like the Republicans in the US, the Coalition's new strategy appears to be to undermine, block, discredit, confuse, attack and hamper at every opportunity."

He gathered a strong office. Its focus was campaigning, not policy. He had Howard's old press secretary Tony O'Leary running communications strategy for the leader and the Coalition front bench. His new chief of staff was Peta Credlin, a tall Victorian who had worked with Nelson and, unhappily, with Turnbull. There were ructions when she arrived. She guarded Abbott's door — he still works with his door shut tight — deciphered his handwriting and travelled everywhere with him. It was all close-knit: Credlin is the wife of Brian Loughnane, the federal director of the Liberal Party. She is a one-woman policy and politics machine. Abbott came to trust her absolutely. Credlin calls herself "the Queen of no." He calls her "the *force majeure*."

Rudd was spooked. Labor strategists believed he would call a double dissolution election in early January to pass the ETS and destroy Abbott. But he baulked. In April he walked away from "the great moral challenge of our time" and Abbott was able to attack him mercilessly for his hypocrisy, indecision and want of courage. Abbott gave Labor no quarter. He exposed the chaos of Labor's free home insulation scheme and attacked Rudd's plans – so similar to his own – to take over the nation's hospitals. He lined up with the miners to attack Rudd's audacious decision to tax their super-profits. But above all, and with the greatest skill, Abbott drove a panic over the boats. He was playing with the old race fears of Australia without a qualm. He was made for the work. Howard gave him his blessing: "Tony has altered the political scene; there's no doubt about that. There's no disrespect to anybody else, but if you don't recognise that, well, you don't recognise anything about Australian politics."

This was the summer of red Speedos. Abbott was seen diving, swimming and scrambling from the surf after yet another ocean swim in his budgie-smugglers. The slang entered the language. Once again he was telling his life story to the press and television to show that he was so much more than a hard-line monarchist Catholic head-kicker. He did not deny his past. "I'm not sure I could truthfully say that I am a vastly different or better man than I was," he told Tom Dusevic. "I hope I am wiser, I'm certainly more experienced. I hope my intuitions are deeper and more subtle than they were." Most urgently Abbott wanted to convince Australia he was female-friendly. That his wife, Margie, was interviewed by the *Women's Weekly* at this time and once or twice went out campaigning emphasised rather than disguised what a lonely political figure Abbott is in that marriage. The political game is not for her. Nor does she share her husband's intense faith: "I'm a Catholic, but I don't go to mass regularly. So I think he is disappointed by that."

The political message was kept simple and hostile. The advice of pundits and senior figures in his own party to get positive was ignored. He brought a Tea Party anger to his task, anger sustained week after week. It struck a chord. He kept his tongue in check, but in May 2010 made one of his most memorable gaffes. Months earlier he had told Neil Mitchell on 3AW that an Abbott government would raise no new taxes. Kerry O'Brien now wanted to know how that squared with the plan to charge business billions to pay for parental leave. "I know politicians are going to be judged on everything they say but sometimes in the heat of discussion you go a little bit further than you would if it was an absolutely calm, considered, prepared, scripted remark," Abbott told the presenter of the ABC's 7.30 Report. "The statements that need to be taken absolutely as gospel truth are those carefully prepared scripted remarks."

Abbott shrugged off the ridicule. He was moving beyond the reach of his critics. In six months he had transformed the fortunes of the Coalition. The party he took over in December 2009 faced a rout, but six months later the polls were saying it was in a position to beat the government. The fall in Rudd's personal popularity in that time was the most dramatic a prime minister had suffered in a decade. But for Abbott, the Coalition parties would not be where they were. Yet he remained stubbornly unpopular. His approval rating was falling in lock-step with Rudd's. The question troubling Abbott's Liberal colleagues was whether this unloved leader could eventually take them across the line.

Rudd was sacked on 24 June. It was a fundamental blunder provoked by Abbott's success. Howard rang his protégé: "You have achieved the greatest prize that any Opposition leader can: you have secured the scalp of a prime minister." Julia Gillard's lead in the polls lasted a month. Even her big lead with women evaporated. She called an election for 21 August. Abbott reduced his stump speech to a lethal fifteen words: "End the waste, pay back the debt, stop the new taxes and stop the boats." For the best part of a year, Labor tacticians had been waiting for Abbott to fall apart. They were sure he would finally come undone in the campaign. It didn't happen. There were no Bernie Banton moments. And on election night Abbott thought he had pulled off the first defeat of a first-term government since the Depression. Labor won more votes but the Coalition won more seats. Dissatisfaction with both Abbott and Gillard had led to the election of four Independents and one Green in the House of Representatives. All Abbott had to do was talk a few of them across and the prize was his.

But he couldn't. He had never wanted to look like a prime minister in waiting before and didn't now. Gillard moved swiftly and negotiated strategically. Abbott held back too long and then came in too hard. Tony Windsor was perhaps his best bet. Windsor doesn't think Abbott all bad: a good health minister, fit and hard-working. "But Tony Abbott is still at university in terms of the way he does stuff. I think it's his style. There's a number of them on both sides that live that life. They are still there." Abbott took Windsor and Rob Oakeshott for granted in the early days of the negotiations, but Windsor says the bravado didn't last. "You know he portrays himself as the man of the moment, the man of great strength, physical strength. But during part of that period it was quite pitiful." Windsor thought Abbott would even have agreed to a carbon tax if that would make him prime minister. "I quite believe him when he said, 'I'll do anything to get this job, anything other than sell my arse.' And he said he'd really have to think hard about that. He wasn't joking. He was desperate. That was at the stage where it was quite pitiful."

Gillard was sworn in and so began what might be the strangest term the national parliament has ever seen. The Opposition was led by a man who believed that at any moment death, scandal or defection could make him prime minister. He was intent on demolishing the government and wrecking the parliament. But it didn't happen, despite the scandals laid on by the Labor Party. The parliament functioned. Gillard survived. Complex legislation was passed. And month in, month out pollsters reported that Australians were loathing it all: minority government, the taxes, the tone of national debate, Gillard and Abbott.

The price Gillard paid for being prime minister was taxing carbon emissions. She had promised she wouldn't and now she was. Abbott threw everything he had into whipping up a "people's revolt" against Gillard: the stunts in car yards and dry-cleaner's shops, the unrestrained hyperbole and the personal endorsements given to dodgy protests outside parliament. In March last year the Sydney shock-jock Chris Smith brought a crowd of about a thousand to Canberra. Pauline Hanson was wandering around. There were nutters and conspiracy theorists everywhere. Abbott brought only the hard right of his front bench with him. "I do not see scientific heretics," Abbott told the cheering crowd. "I do not see environmental vandals, I see people who want honest government." Nor, it seems, did he see the placards denouncing Gillard as "Ju-Liar" or hear the chants of "Ditch the bitch." It was all caught on television. His judgment was in question twice in those days: first for addressing that bizarre rally and then for mocking Gillard for going to the royal wedding: "She may not believe in God, the monarchy or marriage but there will be a royal wedding bounce." In a single sentence he managed to abuse the prime minister, all de facto couples, everyone who doesn't believe in God, and republicans, who make up roughly half the country. But these are not Abbott's people.

Though unable to prevent either the carbon tax or Gillard's watered-down mining tax becoming law, Abbott did manage to drag Labor support down to the lowest level in fifteen years. But he was losing the battle to win the affection of the nation. This was not for want of friends in the press. News Limited had long taken Abbott to its bosom. He was one of them. He had been publishing opinion pieces in News Limited papers for thirty-five years. Most weeks the leader of the Opposition visited Holt Street in Sydney or the *Herald and Weekly Times* in Melbourne. He had become close to the *Australian*'s editor, Chris Mitchell, who had become one of his constituents. Many Saturday nights were spent eating at the Mitchells' in Manly. On talkback radio he spoke directly to his core supporters, what he called "the base." He shied away from interrogations on the 7.30 *Report*, preferring to chew the fat with Alan Jones, Andrew Bolt, Ray Hadley and the team on Channel Nine's *Today Show*. But none of this was winning hearts and minds. "Abbott personally is a very unpopular leader," wrote Peter Hartcher in November 2011. "He has offered himself as the human boot to stamp on the face of the Prime Minister. But it seems that Australians don't want to be led by an angry boot. The polls are telling us that as much as Australia would like to be rid of Gillard, it is loath to replace her with Abbott."

His party room was becoming fractious. There were those who believed Abbott's policy of total opposition wasn't working. The short-term strategy of saying no to so much leaves the Coalition facing the prospect of chaos in government. The taxes he promised to abolish would leave a $70 billion hole for an Abbott government to fill. His economic credentials were coming under sustained attack. For fifteen months he had been driven by the belief that there might be an election any day. But Gillard's government wasn't collapsing. She was unpopular but resilient. Abbott had spooked Rudd, but not her. Wasn't it time, senior Liberals were asking, for the party to change tack? Go positive? Abbott rejected the idea emphatically. He reminded the faint of heart that his strategy had raised the primary vote of the party to a magnificent 48 per cent. The Coalition was poised to rout Labor. He would deliver a series of "headland" speeches in autumn 2012 – on the economy, the environment, the boats, infrastructure and communities – but he would go on doing what he had been doing until the job was finished. He would attack the government's legitimacy and competence; fan fears of boat people; and relentlessly pursue Gillard's "toxic tax based on a lie." He would remain the conundrum at the heart of Australian politics: the deeply unpopular leader of a triumphant Opposition.

If he wished, Abbott could look right out across the landscape of commercial Sydney. The view from his office is a view of power. Around him are the great law firms and the merchant banks of the city. Far below is Chifley Square. The sky is the perfect blue of a Sydney winter day. But he keeps the vertical blinds shut tight. It's puzzling. He hasn't a glimpse of the outside world and no one out there can see him. The lights are blazing. This doesn't have the feel of a room that's much used: Hansards on the shelves and standard-issue furniture. No picture of the Queen. Two souvenirs are the only Abbott touch. One is a painting of Coober Pedy. The other, at eye level when he's sitting at his desk, is an autographed photograph of Aussie Joe Bugner in the ring with Muhammad Ali.

Abbott is bursting out of his shirt. To be face to face with him is to be in the presence of one of the most intriguing contests in Australian politics: Abbott with his own body. Was there ever an Australian politician for whom the body counted so much, who did so much to keep his packet of muscle and bone in trim? Until he was leader of the Opposition he was a mass-a-day man. He once wrote: "The mass was a chance to quietly restore one's energies." Getting to mass isn't always possible now but he works his body six days a week. He's up before dawn for an hour on his bike and maybe later – especially after a gruelling Question Time – he spends some time in the gym. He doesn't win those ocean swims and doesn't see himself as a great competitor. He is in it for the discipline. When the shadowy Father Mankowski introduced him to boxing, it was the discipline young Abbott loved: "The challenge of a new and ferocious discipline naturally had me hooked."

Few love and forgive this man so much as those who played football with him. Peter FitzSimons, journalist and biographer of our national heroes, has had it out with Abbott over gays, climate change, abortion, the republic, asylum seekers and industrial relations. But the affection remains. FitzSimons watched the famous punch-up between coach Abbott and player Joe Hockey in the late 1980s: "a blistering array of uppercuts, hay-makers and wild swings." FitzSimons sees in the politician the young man's love of rugby scrums:

> Abbo never saw a scrum that he didn't like … what he most loved, and I mean this, was doing it when the conditions were *appalling*. One night in June, 1989, it all came together. A howling wind, screaming imprecations at the devil. Sheets of rains without end. A whole *quagmire* of mud to work with. Situation perfect … as we maddened muddy wombats staggered after him. Forty minutes in, as our eyeballs rolled with exhaustion, I dinkum remember looking at his own beatific countenance, all grin and ears, the rain pouring off his uncovered head and having this distinct thought: "I think he's a little bit insane – in a hugely likeable way."

He gave up football in his mid-thirties, about the time he married. He will soon be fifty-five. Few men of that age are pushing themselves through ten hours of triathlon. If he is ever living in Kirribilli House, he won't be taking power walks along the shore in a Vodafone tracksuit. He will be up at 4 a.m. for a fifty-kilometre ride in Lycra. The punishment is necessary. Abbott jokes about this but knows it is true: "If I didn't get regular exercise I'm sure I'd drink more, I might be popping pills, I might be going slightly round the twist."

He is just back from Washington and Beijing, where he delivered a couple of big speeches, both written by himself. The first had the traditional function of reassuring America that the man who is looking every inch the next prime minister is a safe pair of hands. He laid it on thick: "Few Australians would regard America as a foreign country." He passed on the thanks of a grateful nation for the chance to fight side by side with America in Vietnam, Iraq and Afghanistan. He acknowledged America as the guardian of the great traditions of the Western world. The scourge of the boats quoted the "huddled masses" line from the Statue of Liberty. It was all astonishingly banal. Abbott urged his hosts at the Heritage Foundation to bring the nation's debts and deficits under control and not lose faith in themselves: "America needs to believe in itself the way others still believe in it." While he was in the neighbourhood he went to New York for the – surely redundant by now – ceremonial visit of the next prime minister to Rupert Murdoch. Back home in the *Spectator Australia* he laid it on thick again: "Along with the commander of the First AIF, Sir John Monash, and the penicillin inventor, Lord Florey, he is one of the Australians who have made the most difference in the world."

China feted Abbott. The officials he met were high-powered. His was regarded as a visit of importance. His address was not craven. He did not lay it on thick. How many times must Chinese officials have heard Australian dignitaries try to explain this continent's early wretched relationship with the Chinese? They know the truth. Why not speak the truth? Abbott put about as good a spin on it as he could: early Chinese settlers, early Chinese politicians and Chinese restaurants in country towns were "an early sign of our readiness to absorb foreign ways and make them our own." He rightfully claimed the credit for his party for ending the "embarrassment" of White Australia. But there were three tough messages in his breakfast speech to the Australian Chamber of Commerce in Beijing: we will never break with America, China must become free, and Australia is wary of Chinese investment. His real audience at that moment was the National Party back home: "Chinese investment is complicated by the prevalence of state-owned enterprises. It would rarely be in Australia's national interest to allow a foreign government or its agencies to control an Australian business."

Back from the world stage, Abbott is on the road again. That morning he has already been in the western suburbs of Sydney complaining about the impact of the carbon tax on Pirtek Fluid Transfer Solutions. Over the next couple of days he is due to do the same at the Tamar Valley Dairy in Tasmania and Hart Marine on the Mornington Peninsula. Sunday will see him up the coast for the Coffs Coast Cycle Challenge. That's his life. But first, after I'd been trailing him for a couple of months, the time had come for the interview. He would be pithy, funny and illuminating. But he decided I could quote nothing he said. Our talk was off the record. Why? God knows. The one statement he insists I put his name to is this: he can't remember threatening Barbara Ramjan all those years ago at university and believes to have thrown those punches would be out of character. I have done my duty. Of course, everything we discuss is somewhere in this essay. I haven't wasted a scrap.

"The beauty of being leader is you are freer to be yourself," he said a couple of years ago. That's not true. Leadership has made Abbott less himself. The spark has gone out of his writing. Those vast headland speeches were so dreary they made no impact at all. Perhaps that was the point. He thinks more and says less. That remarkable face-off with Channel Seven reporter Mark Riley in February 2011 showed a man winning a superhuman struggle to hold his tongue. His staff are on alert to prevent slips. So is he. Abbott sees himself on a mission for his supporters. In his eyes, half the country at least is depending on him. He mustn't betray the mission. And he is so close. They say Abbott is a patient man but this must be agony. Power is just the other side of the glass. All he has to do, one senior Labor figure told me, is stay vertical.

Whatever might happen under an Abbott government, his victory would perpetuate his kind of Opposition. What worked for him would be done to him. Australia would face the prospect of being locked, for the foreseeable future, into a cycle of hyper-aggressive Opposition. Whether we like it or not – and the polls clearly tell us we don't – it promises to be bare-knuckle time for Australia for a long, long time. Of course, an Abbott win would mean no carbon tax and no mining tax: no reasonable prospect of dealing with global warming and no dividend from what's left of the minerals boom. But an Abbott victory would also lock in the politics of the boats. As I was finishing this essay, Gillard's expert panel recommended, among other things, the reopening of camps on Manus Island and Nauru. Abbott had been demanding that from the day he became leader of the Opposition. Gillard caved in. Abbott's intransigence had paid a huge political dividend. He helped rush the necessary legislation through parliament but was offering no truce: "The point I keep making is if you want John Howard-style results, you have to put in John Howard-style policies." The most likely prospect is that the boats will keep coming under Gillard and under any Abbott government. What then? Abbott would be exposed to all the abuse he heaped on her. Again: what worked for him would be done to him.

The joke goes that Abbott would be the first DLP prime minister of Australia. He wouldn't mind us believing that. He still carries a torch for Santa, and none of the old warrior's other disciples has risen so high on the Liberal side of politics. Ever since he stepped into parliament nearly twenty years ago he has been invoking God and the Catholic values that drive him. They are his political persona. They are the proof that there is depth and humanity to this attack dog. Yet what impact have they had, in the end, on this man's life in power? How much would they drive Tony Abbott, PM? Which Abbott are we going to get when things are tough, I asked him: Values Abbott or Politics Abbott? I wish I could quote his answer. My sense is we'll get the Abbott he decides to give us at any particular time. He is certainly not stepping back from those lessons he said he learnt from the Hewson debacle: you've got to have principles in politics but you've got to finesse them:

> If you have them so strongly, and so dogmatically, that they cause the public to shrink from you in fear, there is a problem. And I'm not saying that you necessarily surrender your principles; but I am saying that you have got to be conscious of the fact that no matter how right your principles are, if they don't resonate with the general public, and you are living in a democratic polity, you've got a problem.

Values Abbott will have his way on some issues because the DLP is also alive and well inside the ALP. Whether he wins or loses, there is no prospect in this country of gay marriage, drug reform, euthanasia, a republic or a bill of rights. The last on the list he regards as a complete waste of time. Win or lose, nothing will be done to roll back abortion rights because Politics Abbott knows that's simply not possible. Values Abbott will work to cushion families from the realities of economic life. And if the Coalition parties allow him, Values Abbott will protect working men and women from the full force of the labour market. But he won't put his career on the line for any of this. He won't abandon his old DLP principles, but he won't be a martyr to them either.

The Abbott that matters is Politics Abbott. That's the one who got him where he is today: an aggressive populist with a sharp tongue; a political animal with lots of charm; a born protégé with ambitions to lead; a big brain but no intellectual; a bluff guy who proved a more than competent minister; a politician with little idea what he might do if he ever got to the top; and a man profoundly wary of change. His values have never stood in his way. In the past he has talked about being prime minister to make a difference, to allow Australians to be their better selves and – again and again and again – to ensure a more cohesive society. I asked him why he wanted the job. He had an answer but he won't let me say what it was.

Anything can happen in politics in a year. Abbott's party is hoping his strategy of total war will last the distance. And they are hoping, sometime soon, we might come to like this man. If we don't, he will be asking us to do something we've never done before: replace a government we don't like with a leader we don't like either. Somehow all those frank interviews over the years haven't done the trick. Nor has Pollie Pedal or the ocean swims or the volunteer fire brigade. He looks terrific fixing sheds up in Aurukun for Aboriginal kids, but a few days later he's back in parliament snarling. He's out at another factory raging against Gillard's lies and the crippling carbon tax. He's a worker. No doubt about that. But the point of it all is power. Without power it's been a waste of time.

20 *August* 2012

SOURCES

This essay is built on the work of dozens of my colleagues over many years. I thank them. I thank Tony Abbott and his staff for the help they gave. I thank the politicians and bureaucrats, named and unnamed, who shared their experiences with me. My particular thanks go to Rebecca Giggs, who was my ferocious researcher and sounding board. And first to last my thanks to Sebastian Tesoriero.

1	Polling material on Abbott as at end July 2012: Essential.
2	"God almighty": *Age*, 2 December 2009, p. 1.
2	"I accept at times": *Australian*, 2 December 2009, p. 7. See also p. 1 of the *Age* and p. 4 of the *Sydney Morning Herald* for that day.
3	"These usually": Tony Abbott, *Battlelines*, Melbourne University Press, Melbourne, 2009, p. 7.
3	"*Gallipoli*" etc: *Sunday Age*, 6 December 2009, p. 5.
3	"A Don Quixote": Peter Costello, *The Costello Memoirs*, Melbourne University Press, Melbourne, 2009, p. 55.
4	Polling material on Abbott as at the second week of August: Newspoll, 7 August 2012.
6	"He was wild": *Sydney Morning Herald*, Spectrum, 11 March 2000, p. 1.
6	"Most students will be interested": *Democrat*, 22 March 1976.
7	"His mother and I knew pretty early on": *Australian*, 21 August 2010, p. 10.
7	"Even in those days": Channel Nine, *Sunday*, 15 July 2001.
7	"Sir John, this must be frightfully boring": there are many versions of this story. According to Lenore Taylor in the *Australian Financial Review*, 30 April 2004, p. 28, Abbott was suggesting a Labor rally but Abbott in *Battlelines*, p. 8, says it was a Liberal rally.
7	"Fantastic!": *Sydney Morning Herald*, 4 November 1995, p. 26.
8	"I first met him": Channel Nine, *Sunday*, 15 July 2001.
8	"the most important male influence": *Australian*, 2 December 2009, p. 13.
8	"Some instinct whispered": *Age*, 30 January 2007, p. 13.
9	"It was a thrill": *Battlelines*, p. 11.
9	"I have been under the Santamaria spell": *Age*, 30 January 2007, p. 13.
9	"The greatest living Australian": *Hansard*, 3 March 1998, p. 248.
9	"A philosophical star": *Hansard*, 3 March 1998, p. 248.
10	"His real role": *Daily Telegraph*, 26 February 1998, p. 4.
10	"This organisation has a long history": *Honi Soit*, 28 February 1977, p. 4.
10	"As an infrequently practising": *University of Sydney News*, "Election of Student

Fellows of Senate," 1976, p. 184.

10   "He came down to the SRC": *Honi Soit*, 28 February 1977, p. 4.

11   "Tony was a warm": Bullock to me.

11   "It was as necessary to break": Patrick Morgan (ed.), *B.A. Santamaria: Running the Show: Selected Documents 1939–1999*, Miegunyah Press, Melbourne, 2008, pp. 373–4.

12   "The present crop": B.A. Santamaria, *Santamaria: A Memoir*, Oxford University Press, Melbourne, 1997, p. 266.

13   "I ACCUSE": *Weekend Australian*, 29 January 1977, p. 21.

14   "She was infatuated": *Bulletin*, 1 March 2005, p. 23.

14   "I loved uni": *Sydney Morning Herald*, Good Weekend, 14 April 2006, p. 22.

14   "I decided" and "I just wasn't ready": *Bulletin*, 1 March 2005, p. 24.

15   "When AUS champions": *Democrat*, 12 May 1977.

16   "Why don't you smile" and "I jumped back": *Daily Telegraph*, 12 January 1978, p. 4.

16   "She was speaking": *Daily Telegraph*, 13 January 1978, p. 5.

16   "But no": Ramjan to me.

17   "At times it was": *Bulletin*, 4–5 June 1994, p. 10.

17   "The leading light": 7 February 1978, p. 19.

18   "unprovoked and unnecessary": SRC minutes, 27 June 1978.

19   "Tony settled on a plan": *The Costello Memoirs*, pp. 54–5.

20   "senseless, futile and provocative": *Cue*, 3 October 1978, authorised by Jeremy Jones and Paul Brereton.

20   "newly elected president": *Sydney Morning Herald*, 22 September 1978, p. 1.

20   "Luckily, it is lunchtime": *Honi Soit*, 9 April 1979, p. 6.

21   "This is a man's room": *Honi Soit*, 23 July 1979, p. 3.

21   "Marxists realised": Nationwide, 20 March 1979, www.youtube.com/watch?v=-CbRpxd3_EH0&feature=player_embedded.

21   "All physical objects": *Honi Soit*, 5 March 1979, p. 4.

22   "The SRC is unnecessary": SRC minutes, 30 May 1978.

22   "the Active Defence": letter of 29 October 1979, reproduced in University of Sydney Senate Minutes, 5 November 1975, pp. 957–8.

22   "Otherwise high-handed": *University of Sydney News*, 2 October 1979, p. 136.

22   "moral force of character": from the terms of Rhodes' will, www.rhodeshouse.ox.ac.uk/page/about.

22   "Second-grade footballer": source to me.

23   "extreme causes": *Sydney Morning Herald*, 22 November 1980, p. 4.

23   "It belonged to me": *Battlelines*, pp. 7–8.

23   "I loved my time": ABC Radio National, *Grandstand*, 22 June 2012.

26   "The RSPCA is one of Australia's": www.liberal.org.au/Latest-News/2012/
      06/26/Tony-Abbott-doorstop-interview.aspx.
26   "I can tell": *Sydney Morning Herald*, 27 June 2012, p. 6.
27   "But I found it difficult": *Bulletin*, 18 August 1987, p. 62.
27   "I doubt" and "both the embodiment": *Battlelines*, p. 14.
27   "He wanted to be": ABC *Four Corners*, "The Authentic Mr Abbott," 19 March 2010.
27   "We were all just horrified" and "It's what he's": *Sydney Morning Herald*, Good
      Weekend, 14 April 2006, p. 22.
28   "Tony came to the seminary": *Sydney Morning Herald*, Spectrum, 11 March 2000,
      p. 1.
28   "He wasn't so much a big fish": *Courier Mail*, 5 April 1997, p. 24.
28   "As time went by": *Australian*, 13 June 1984, p. 11.
29   "Tony wasn't one": Debien to me.
29   "St Patrick's is a microcosm": *Sydney Morning Herald*, 26 September 1985, p. 64.
30   "Three years' grinding": *Bulletin*, 18 August 1987, p. 58.
30   "serving a local": *Australian*, Magazine, 13 December 2003, p. 18.
30   "political love child": *Australian*, Magazine, 13 December 2003, p. 18.
31   "Very intelligent": ABC *Four Corners*, "The Authentic Mr Abbott," 19 March 2010.
31   "He would make": Kennedy to me.
31   "I was attracted": *Australian Financial Review*, 4 December 2009, p. 62.
32   "He had called": *News Weekly*, 20 December 2008, p. 13.
32   "In twenty-five years": *Sydney Morning Herald*, 15 June 1991, p. 21.
32   "who keeps very": *Sydney Morning Herald*, 16 August 1990, p. 26.
33   "In any street": *Age*, 9 September 1992, p. 15.
33   "He was one of the most": ABC *Four Corners*, "The Authentic Mr Abbott," 19 March
      2010.
33   "While I always": *Australian Financial Review*, 4 December 2009, p. 62.
33   "political and communications": *Australian Financial Review*, 11 February 1992, p. 5.
33–34 "How can you sacrifice," "If you don't," "The art of effective" and "Unless
      you're in": *News Weekly*, 20 December 2008, pp. 12–14.
35   "We have always believed": *Hansard*, 27 June 2012, p. 8222.
35   "This matter turns": *Hansard*, 27 June 2012, p. 8232.
36   "We did try hard today": www.tonyabbott.com.au/LatestNews/InterviewTran-
      scripts/tabid/85/articleType/ArticleView/articleId/8771/Joint-Press-Confer-
      ence-Parliament-House-Canberra.aspx.
36   "key Liberal party strategist": *Sydney Morning Herald*, 18 December 2010, p. 6.
37   "He put it on the table": *Sydney Morning Herald*, News Review, 19 February 2011,
      p. 9.

37 "It works incredibly": *Courier Mail*, 24 February 2011, p. 32.

37 Poll on who is to blame for the stalemate: Nielsen, *Sydney Morning Herald*, 2 July 2012, p. 4.

37 Poll on level of anxiety about the boats: the Lowy Institute's *Australia and the World, Public Opinion and Foreign Policy*, 2011, p. 14.

37 Poll on policies too soft or too harsh: Essential online polls for April–May 2009 and October 2010.

37 Poll backing to reintroduce Pacific Solution: Nielsen, *Age*, 7 June 2010, p. 2.

38 "This very possessed" and "We never looked back": Waddy to me.

40 "There is no reason" and "The issue is": *Australian*, 31 May 1990, p. 8.

40 "I had been altogether": *Australian*, Magazine, 13 December 2003, p. 18.

41 "a very good": *Sydney Morning Herald*, 19 February 1994, p. 3.

42 "reclaiming our political": *Battlelines*, p. 20.

42 "who sparked my interest," "the contemporary politician" and "May God": *Hansard*, 31 May 1994, p. 1080.

42 "junkyard dog": *Sydney Morning Herald*, 28 March 1994, p. 4.

42 "Political horsepower": *Australian*, Magazine, 13 December 2003, p. 18.

42 "Abbott's concerns": Channel Nine, *Sunday*, 15 July 2001. This allegation was also put by Richard Flanagan and denied by Abbott in the *Age*, 31 March 2001, p. 5.

43 "He's a dangerous": *Sydney Morning Herald*, 17 June 1998, p. 12.

43 "My view was" and "So there was never": *Sydney Morning Herald*, News Review, 30 August 2003, p. 30.

44 "Misleading the ABC": *Sydney Morning Herald*, Spectrum, 11 March 2000, p. 1.

44 "Abbott and Costello": Bob Ellis, *Goodbye Jerusalem: Night Thoughts of a Labor Outsider*, first printing, Random House, Sydney, pp. 472–3.

45 "weak and unreliable": statement of claim quoted in the *Age*, 24 October 1998, p. 1.

45 "Under modern adoption": *Courier Mail*, 5 April 1997, p. 24.

46 "What will you say": www.tonyabbott.com.au/News/tabid/94/articleType/ArticleView/articleId/8780/Interview-with-David-Speers-Sky-News.aspx.

46 Abbott a coward: *Australian*, 9 July 2012, p. 7.

47 "What you've got": ABC *Four Corners*, "The Authentic Mr Abbott," 19 March 2010.

47 "It's going to be": *Sydney Morning Herald*, 5 June 2012, p. 1.

47 "It will make every job" etc: from various interviews on 1 to 4 July to be found at www.tonyabbott.com.au/LatestNews.aspx.

48 "This is an important local manufacturer": www.tonyabbott.com.au/News/tabid/94/articleType/ArticleView/articleId/8796/Joint-Doorstop-Interview-Central-Coast-New-South-Wales.aspx.

48   Polls: *Sydney Morning Herald*, 30 July 2012, p. 1.

48   "voters are highly sceptical": *Australian Financial Review*, 16 July 2012, p. 11.

49   "My department": source to me.

49   "On my first day": *Battlelines*, p. 47.

51   "It takes considerable": *Sydney Morning Herald*, 31 December 1999, p. 11.

51   "perilously close": *Sunday Herald Sun*, 10 September 2000, p. 16.

52   "Organisations should not": *Australian*, 15 September 2000, p. 33.

53   "It's okay": Michael Kirby, *A Private Life: Fragments, Memories, Friends*, Allen & Unwin, Sydney, 2011. p. 110.

53   "Tony Abbott wrote": *Michael Kirby, Paradoxes and Principles*. Federation Press, Sydney, 2011, p. 317.

53   "a bit threatened": Channel Nine, *60 Minutes*, 5 March 2010.

53   "challenges orthodox": ABC *Lateline*, 8 March 2010.

53   "intrinsic moral evil": *On the Pastoral Care of Homosexual Persons*, letter to the Congregation for the Doctrine of the Faith, paragraph 3.

54   "ethnic cleansing": *Sydney Morning Herald*, 2 September 1999, p. 7.

54   "telling whoppers": *Age*, 20 October 1999, p. 19.

54   "proxy war": *Australian Financial Review*, 18 January 1999, p. 2.

54   "Clearly explain how": *Sydney Morning Herald*, 16 October 1999, p. 1.

55   "We can't stop": *Sydney Morning Herald*, 10 July 2001, p. 3, quoting ABC *Four Corners*.

56   "This idea that" and "Every Australian needs": *Australian*, Magazine, 13 December 2003, p. 18.

56   "instrument for giving": *Hansard*, 31 May 1994, p. 1080.

56   "You know what": ABC *Lateline*, 14 July 2011.

56–57 Western civilisation.

        "an essential part": *Age*, Opinion, 14 June 2001, p. 17.

        "scientific and cultural": address to CIS Consilium "The West and its Challenges," 8 August 2003.

        "We don't support": *Australian*, Opinion, 4 August 2003, p. 9.

        "the oldest continuing": *Age*, Opinion, 20 October 1999, p. 19.

        "to uphold universal": *Battlelines*, p. 158.

        "the whole edifice" and "the presumption of": *Australian*, Magazine, 14 June 2008, p. 14.

        "fundamental to": *Hansard*, 21 August 2002, p. 5303.

        "The question haunting": *Australian*, Magazine, 14 June 2008, p. 14.

58   "He showed a great": Helen Coonan to me.

58   "Ian Hickie": *Sydney Morning Herald*, News Review, 7 August 2010, p. 1.

59   "a perfectly good" and "Power divided": speech to the Young Liberals'

National Conference reported in the *Australian*, 25 January 2005, p. 13.

59   "Eventually he was" and "He wasn't ruthless": source to me.

60   "If we hadn't": Peter Hartcher, *To the Bitter End*, Allen & Unwin, Sydney, 2009, p. 52.

60   "The problem with": from "The Ethical Responsibilities of a Christian Politi-cian," 16 March 2004, www.tonyabbott.com.au/LatestNews/Speeches/tabid/88/articleType/ArticleView/articleId/3550/THE-ETHICAL-RESPONSI-BILITIES-OF-A-CHRISTIAN-POLITICIAN.aspx.

61   "He's just too right-wing": *Courier Mail*, 20 March 2004, p. 37.

62   "Margie and my daughters": *Bulletin*, 1 March 2005, p. 21.

62   "I'm sorry that poor": *Age*, 22 March 2005, p. 1.

62   "Right at the end": Coonan to me.

63   "Never one to be": *The Costello Memoirs*, p. 55.

63   "You have given": *Daily Telegraph*, 22 August 2005, p. 2.

64   "A catastrophic political": *Battlelines*, pp. 25–6.

64   "It was always": *To the Bitter End*, p. 81.

64   "There is no one Catholic": *Australian*, 21 August 1998, p. 1.

65   "moral snobbery" and "Finding fault": *Australian*, 23 April 1998, p. 13.

65   "A political argument": *Age*, 12 October 2007, p. 9.

66   "Political leadership": *Battlelines*, pp. 42–3.

67   "We were in parallel universes": *The Costello Memoirs*, p. 251.

67   "Abbott thought": *The Costello Memoirs*, p. 250.

67   "From the very beginning": ABC *Four Corners*, "The Authentic Mr Abbott," 19 March 2010.

67   "You can't even get here": ABC *Lateline*, 31 October 2007.

67   "Look, it was a stunt": *Sydney Morning Herald*, 31 October 2007.

68   "the very best of good": *Australian*, 26 November 2007, p. 12.

70–72 "You will see them" and "I often talk" and "you are people": Address to the Western Sydney Seats Launch and the Carbon Tax Rally, Parramatta, Sydney, 8 July 2012, www.tonyabbott.com.au/LatestNews/Speeches/tabid/88/articleType/ArticleView/articleId/8803/Address-to-the-Western-Sydney-Seats-Launch-and-the-Carbon-Tax-Rally-Parramatta-Sydney.aspx.

70   "Only the most" and "a type of marriage": *Battlelines*, p. 177.

71   "Sometimes it is better": *Australian Financial Review*, 10 March 2010, p. 9.

71   "middle-income families": *Hansard*, 31 May 1994, p. 1080.

73   "Don't you think": Radio 2GB, 2 November 2009.

73   "It's a plausible": *Australian*, 24 July 2009, p. 12.

73   "absolute crap": *Pyrenees Advocate*, 2 October 2009, p. 5.

74   "his constant changes": Lenore Taylor & David Uren, *Shitstorm: Inside Labor's Darkest Days*, Melbourne University Press, p. 190.
74   "this constant message": "The Ethical Responsibilities of a Christian Politician," 16 March 2004, www.tonyabbott.com.au/LatestNews/Speeches/tabid/88/articleType/ArticleView/articleId/3550/THE-ETHICAL-RESPONSIBILITIES-OF-A-CHRISTIAN-POLITICIAN.aspx.
75   "This will be the making of him": ABC 7.30 *Report*, 6 December 2007.
76   "a fundamental crisis": *Australian*, 7 February 2009, p. 23.
76   "the national government": *Australian*, 12 November 2008, p. 14.
76   "meek, shy": *Australian*, Magazine, 14 June 2008, p. 14. Abbott was quoting an unnamed writer in the *New York Times*.
76   "I was none": *Australian*, Magazine, 20 March 2010, p. 14.
77   "The Labor Party": *Australian*, 27 June 2009, p. 5.
77–78 Polling for preferred Liberal leader: Nielsen poll, *Sydney Morning Herald*, 30 November 2009, p. 1. The figures were Hockey 36 per cent, Turnbull 32 per cent and Abbott 20 per cent.
79   "When Winston Churchill": *Battlelines*, p. 187.
81   "It would seem": Sir Robert Menzies, *The Measure of the Years*, Coronet Books, London, 1970, p. 22.
81   "Like the Republicans": *Sunday Age*, 28 March 2010, p. 19.
82   "Queen of no" and "*force majeure*": *Australian*, Magazine, 5 November 2011, p. 12.
82   "Tony has altered": ABC *Four Corners*, "The Authentic Mr Abbott," 15 March 2010.
82   "I'm not sure": *Australian*, Magazine, 20 March 2010, p. 14.
82   "I'm a Catholic": *Women's Weekly*, February 2010, p. 24.
83   "I know politicians": *Herald Sun*, 18 May 2010, p. 2.
83   "You have achieved": *Sunday Age*, 27 June 2010, p. 4.
84   "But Tony Abbott is": Windsor to me.
85   "I do not see": *Age*, 24 March 2011, p. 1.
85   "She may not": *Sydney Morning Herald*, 23 March 2011, p. 4.
86   "Abbott personally": *Sydney Morning Herald*, 26 November 2011, p. 9.
87   "The mass": *Bulletin*, 18 August 1987, p. 59.
87   "The challenge": *Battlelines*, p. 14.
88   "a blistering array": *Sydney Morning Herald*, 3 November 2001, p. 81.
88   "Abbo never saw": *Sun Herald*, Sport, 22 August 2010, p. 6.
88   "If I didn't": *Sun Herald*, 5 December 2010, p. 30.
88–89 "Few Australians" and other references to the 18 July 2012 address to the Heritage Foundation: www.tonyabbott.com.au/LatestNews/Speeches/tabid/88/

articleType/ArticleView/articleId/8816/Address-to-the-Heritage-Foundation-Washington-DC.aspx.

89   "Along with": *Spectator Australia*, 28 July 2012, p. ix.

89   "an early sign" and other references to the 24 July 2012 address to the Australian Chamber of Commerce, Beijing: www.tonyabbott.com.au/LatestNews/Speeches/tabid/88/articleType/ArticleView/articleId/8818/Address-to-AustCham-Beijing-China.aspx.

90   "The beauty of being": *Sydney Morning Herald*, News Review, 10 April 2010, p. 1.

91   "The point": *Courier Mail*, 16 August 2012, p. 9.

91   "If you have": *News Weekly*, 20 December 2008, p. 13.

John Wanna

The social commentator Bernard Salt wrote recently that "politicians should jump on board the disability issue." He was spruiking the swinging votes that might conceivably be changed if politicians heeded the plight of people with disabilities and their long-suffering families. He reported figures from the latest census showing that 1 million people – a sizeable slice of the community – disclosed disabilities requiring assistance with mobility, household care or communication. His main message was that this group was a vital demographic that both sides of politics should ignore at their peril. Governments should shower promises on this substantial group and their carer families to win them "on board."

Separately, in an article on baby boomers being the "sandwiched generation" (looking after both kids and aged parents simultaneously), Dr Lisel O'Dwyer, a demographer from Adelaide University, reported the findings from a survey of 612 baby boomers over the age of fifty. They were beginning to feel the onerous burden of looking after their adult children (and perhaps becoming grand-parents themselves) while still caring for their own frail, aged parents. The *Sydney Morning Herald*'s reporter Julie Power summarised O'Dwyer's observations this way:

> Boomers often helped parents with paperwork and bookkeeping, took them shopping or to doctor's appointments and did house-work for them. They didn't resent doing these jobs, which she esti-mated saved the government billions in assistance, but they did dislike having to help parents with toileting and personal care, which they felt the government should provide.

This statement struck me as "passing strange," to use an anachronistic Rudd-ism. Almost bizarre. We are apparently quite happy to take responsibility for doing the nice bits of caring for family members (perhaps visiting regularly and providing company, reading to them, doing errands and shopping, helping with medications), but somehow governments should take responsibility for the not-so-nice bits of care – the toileting and cleaning!

I do not see *why* this responsibility necessarily falls to government, why it should fall only to government or why other more creative options are not even considered. As a nation we are becoming too quick to pass responsibility to government for any inconvenience, any mishap, any onerous duty, any disaster that happens to strike or any untoward event we dislike. Government in Australia's settlement was traditionally placed as the risk-bearer of last resort; but increasingly it is being considered the option of first resort. And, to go back to the example above, to say that the government should provide personal care merely means that someone else (probably someone unskilled and on low pay) will have to do the unpleasantries.

Both Salt and O'Dwyer expose a political logic Laura Tingle is fundamentally worried about – our predilection for regarding government as a huge milch cow (à la Bentham and Hancock) that endlessly provides for the herd. Or, to use another metaphor, we have come to view government as a giant slot machine, which we keep playing, hoping to cascade regular winnings or benefits. This view has become chronic and debilitating.

Laura Tingle has done us a great service in convincingly sketching out the underlying conditions of the current policy malaise in her essay *Great Expectations*. She canvasses familiar arguments about Australia's historic protectionism (which despite the rhetoric has not gone!); about economic and social expectations that government will come to the rescue; and about how, even in more liberal times, governments still operate from a mentality that they can "fix all." Tingle traces our *default* dependencies on state paternalism, with governments anxious to oblige, but, interestingly, she adds the argument that no amount of government largesse ever satisfies us; the more we ask of government, and the more it gives, the angrier it makes us and the more we want. We are an "angry nation."

From her special vantage point, observing federal politics up close from the press gallery, Tingle wishes to expose (and then change) the impulsive electoral mood that favours instant gratification, but is mixed with complacency, disillusionment and above all else anger. She believes we have been conditioned by our politicians to expect something *all the time* from government, at every budget, at every election, at every policy twist and turn. Governments fuel our expectations, which far exceed what governments can now deliver – so we are condemned to complain. And as we complain, governments hand out more salving policies that further heighten our expectations. It's a vicious circle. So, in public policy today, we have extended the old norms of "protection-all-round" to encompass "benefits-all-round" and "compensation-all-round" (and we could go on – "insurance-all-round," "rescue-all-round" etc.). And Tingle believes all this creates and reproduces bad politics, poor and unsustainable public policies, and longer-term miseries as we lose our productivity and competitive edge.

As a critique, Tingle's essay is penetrating and astute, and worthy of serious engagement by the political class of professional politicians, our "virtual" political parties, old-hat lobbyists too stultified to adapt, media commentators who breathlessly cover politics as sport and the wider community valiantly attempting to maintain an interest in public policy. As a solution, it disappoints. How do we make the necessary changes? What changes are needed? How can we reshape ingrained behaviours across the system? How can we rebalance expectations with sound policy provision? And, above all, how do we de-angrify ourselves?

Tingle relies on many puzzling assumptions to construct her critique. First, she constantly works from an assumption that politicians know, or should know, what they are doing. She is evidently frustrated when she recounts examples of them looking diffident, hesitant, unsure or confounded. But perhaps that is the normal state of politics. We are reminded of this at the end of the essay when she talks of policy being "all at sea" – and mentions the sixteenth-century explorer Ferdinand Magellan, who travelled some 12,600 miles over uncharted waters to reach the mid-Pacific amid mutinies and shipwrecks. She says, "like Magellan, we've reached the end of the known world in our political discussion." Her metaphor reminds us of the powerful image of modern politics conjured up by the famous political philosopher Michael Oakeshott. Oakeshott suggested we "sail a boundless and bottomless sea; there is neither harbour for shelter nor floor for anchorage, neither starting-place nor appointed destination. The enterprise is to keep afloat on an even keel." But it was not a lament; he felt he was accurately representing our political activity.

So to lambast today's mediocre politicians, like Julia Gillard, Wayne Swan, Tony Abbott and Joe Hockey, for not having vision and not knowing what they are doing is maybe to miss the point. They are merely the current crop of deck-hands swabbing while we float on the boundless and bottomless sea. When Ross Garnaut handed an economic report to Bob Hawke in 1983 that advocated deregulation and de-protection and went entirely against Labor policy, Hawke adopted it in the absence of any better options. But did he know how it would turn out? The entire Labor cabinet (which then included some talent) was unsure what floating the dollar would mean and what the consequences would be on selected industries. The industry minister, John Button, said something along the lines of "Oh, shit!" as he heard the news on the way to the airport. Hawke went for it and, as it happened, it turned out quite well. Similarly, even with a less spectacular policy change such as the introduction of the GST (a moderate consolidation), John Howard and Peter Costello had little idea what inflation would occur, how much it would raise, what effects it would have on businesses and how many votes they might subsequently lose. It seems politicians almost routinely make decisions without knowing the consequences – the list is endless: carbon tax, mining rent tax, baby bonus, Pink Batts insulation, BER spending, Fair Work or WorkChoices legislation, health insurance etc.

Secondly, Tingle invites us to believe that Australians have high and insatiable expectations and are regularly disillusioned when these are not met. The weight of these expectations causes politicians to dangle policy bribes in front of us with predictable regularity. But are we certain that people have such high expectations? Most polling on issues suggests that three major issues are of concern to voters: the state of the economy (jobs); their health and that of their dependants; and the education of their kids. Occasionally the environment pops up but goes down again if any economic vulnerabilities appear. Things like personal benefits, social welfare, cash bonuses or lists of entitlements do not appear so salient. Moreover, we know that most people who are relatively satisfied with their circumstances will not make much noise; but those who aren't will bleat. So, to listen to those who feel we are "only getting the downside" of being part of the global economy privileges the views of the complainants, which may distort our assessments. It is not clear to me that people *expected* a baby bonus, *expected* school bonuses, *expected* annual tax cuts that paid for a cup of coffee or even *expected* compensation for the carbon tax. The politicians threw out these goodies largely for their own purposes, nervous that voters might not stay with them. Crass expediency may be driven by politicians rather than by electoral expectations. And moreover, it is far easier for federal ministries, often awash with cash but constricted in their spending, to trigger such cash hand-outs.

Thirdly, Australia, like Canada and New Zealand, inherited British notions of parliamentary control over public funds – which means in reality the ministry's control over all spending. We accepted unquestioningly that we needed to establish a consolidated pool of funds (consolidated revenue) out of which all spending would be made (bar any borrowing). Historically, such notions dated back to the king's purse, a generic repository for the Crown's estate and income. But having a consolidated fund implies we have sitting there each year a big bucket of indiscriminate funds available to be allocated to any supposedly worthy cause. Out of this fund come aged pensions, hospital funding, cash bonuses, portfolio spending, defence and aid money. The fund can be used as a plaything of the current crop of politicians. An alternative and arguably more responsible way of financing public policies is to adopt a more hypothecated approach whereby parliaments establish dedicated independent funds, which are maintained by contributions that cannot be tampered with by politicians. So, for example, many European nations have separate contributory schemes for pensions, unemployment benefits, health insurance, pharmaceuticals and housing, whereby each contributor has "paid in" and enjoys an ownership of a certain level of entitlement. Politics in these nations focuses on deliberating what level of contributions is necessary to deliver the standards of care or benefits the community elects. These nations have often more generous public provision than we are used to, but have far less of the "slot machine" attitude to politics.

Finally, Tingle's history of Australian public policy trajectories focuses almost entirely on the federal story. She covers national politics and so perhaps the explanation for her narrative comes down to her proximity. However, federal politics is rather unusual from a wider perspective. It is a government with historically very limited responsibilities, but increasingly with more ambitious policy appetites, and, most importantly, with huge amounts of cash from its many sources of revenue. It can devote many millions and even billions to particular causes that take its fancy. This factor impacts enormously on federal politics, federal election campaigns and ministerial proclivities. Yet in Australia most "government" is at the state and local levels. The states employ some 1.2 million people in combined workforces compared to the Commonwealth's 160,000 – and most of these federal public servants are located in a few large agencies such as the Tax Office, Centrelink and Immigration. Most of the government services we get beyond cash benefits are provided by state and local governments. Their work is more about managing huge policy responsibilities and big public organisations delivering health, education, safety, land management, water and so on. They have a fraction of the spare cash that the Commonwealth can rustle up; and so their politics is different. State politics is more about relative competencies, scandals in service delivery and waiting lists. So while Tingle's critique is directed towards government more generically, in reality it is a critique of federal politics – of a level of government that is generally disconnected from policy delivery and implementation, yet continues to believe it can initiate whatever new policy agendas it considers we ought to have. Such activity does not imply federal governments "know what they are doing," merely that they remain trapped in their conventions of keeping the ship afloat and sometimes on an even keel.

John Wanna

Mark McKenna

Laura Tingle's essay is a sorely needed contribution to our political debate. At a time when the electorate's cynicism towards all things political shows no sign of abating, we are in dire need of political analysis that takes a wider, historical perspective. Like the best polemics, Tingle's essay is provocative and raises more questions than it answers. She draws out the big paradox: at the same time as rampant privatisation has seen government withdraw from the public sphere, a historically entrenched culture of state paternalism has continued to fuel unrealistic expectations of entitlement in the electorate. From the mid-1990s, the Howard government and the Rudd–Gillard governments have both failed to challenge these perceptions. If anything, they have strengthened them. A generation of Australians has grown accustomed to thinking that the role of government in so-called difficult times is to dispense cash hand-outs and compensation payments. And Tingle is right: Australians must reconceive what we expect of government. Just how and when this readjustment might take place she doesn't say. Rewriting our constitution and having the courage to reform state–federal relations would surely be a good starting point.

While I agree with much of Tingle's analysis, there were a few throwaway lines and over-egged arguments that deserve a response. First to the history: "we spent much of our first century," claims Tingle, "with our politics focused on begging for favours or freedoms from a foreign parliament." In fact, colonial Australians did not "beg" for their freedoms; they demanded them. And far from being an obstacle to our independence, the British were often astonished that we did not take the step much earlier. Moreover, in the nineteenth century the vast majority of Australians did not perceive the British parliament as a "foreign" power. Tingle has read her contemporary view of Britain back onto the past.

And despair though we might at the current state of Australian politics, at several moments in her essay Tingle seems unduly pessimistic. "Beyond military service," she argues, "there is no deeply entrenched value ascribed to doing something for our country, or government." Is the situation really so bleak? Thousands of Australians daily participate in volunteer work of all kinds. Governments and community organisations do acknowledge their contributions, although perhaps not nearly as often as they should. Many other citizens contribute to public and policy debate because they are committed to securing benefits for the common good. Of course, what constitutes "doing something for your country" is very much in the eye of the beholder. Tingle then declares that "Government is rarely portrayed in any of our conversations as a force for good." Again, this is overstated. Take the most glaring examples to the contrary: John Howard's gun laws in the wake of the Port Arthur massacre, Kevin Rudd's apology to the stolen generations, the recent push for a National Disability Insurance Scheme and the impending referendum on constitutional recognition of indigenous Australians. Despite the degree of negativity in much of our political debate, government is still seen as the potential agent of social justice and national renewal. This "faith" in government lies at the core of our democracy. Things are rarely quite as bad as they seem when seen from the Canberra press gallery.

At the core of Tingle's essay is her assertion that "in the failure to break down the habits of state paternalism we have the seeds of much of our modern national anger." Two problems arise here. First, the term "national anger" seems to me an exaggerated and over-simplified description of the mood of our electorate. Anger alone will not suffice. Words like complacent, self-satisfied, misinformed, unreflective, disillusioned and cynical might all serve as more accurate descriptors at certain points in time. Yes, some of us are angry. But this anger is often fuelled by the worst elements of the media: shock-jocks, sensationalist "current affairs" television, and op-ed columnists banging their partisan drums of war and discontent. This raises the second problem with Tingle's argument. In seeking to explain the malaise in the electorate she slates everything home to the history of state paternalism. What she fails to examine is the more contemporary explanation of her national anger. Tingle complains that the new social media amplify the anger in our public discourse. Is it only the social media? What of the media's role more generally? This is what's missing from Tingle's account. She is understandably reticent to place her own profession under the same harsh light of examination that she applies to politicians.

One of the most profound reasons for the electorate's disillusion with politics lies in the mistrust of political information. Political parties in liberal democracies throughout the world are involved in a constant information war. The participants – politicians, journalists and media advisers – are deeply cynical about and suspicious of one another. Every morning the prime minister's advisers rise before dawn to scan the papers and plan their media strategy for the day ahead. Using spin and constant repetition of often mindless and predictable grabs, they attempt to control their party's political direction and ensure that their leaders stay "on message." As politicians try to control the media agenda, so journalists try to puncture this control. Politicians complain that journalists refuse to focus on issues of substance and policy. Journalists complain that politicians rarely speak the truth, refuse to answer questions and avoid addressing issues in public which convulse their party rooms in private – leadership speculation being the prime example. For the audience, this constant cat-and-mouse game can become extremely tedious, feeding disillusion. Our political discourse becomes scripted, repetitive and predictable. Journalists often fail to reflect on the consequences of their own cynicism, just as politicians fail to appreciate the virtues of leaving their media-massaged statements on the cutting-room floor and speaking spontaneously, honestly and naturally.

Together with a marked deterioration in the civility of political debate (a trend identified in many other democracies) we have also witnessed a rapid decline in the cultural authority of politicians. In democratising our civic discourse, the media have eroded the respect and deference that was once shown to politicians while at the same time making them more accessible and accountable. For a graphic demonstration of what has happened to the cultural authority of politicians we need look no further than ABC TV's *Q&A*.

Here, amidst the cacophony of live audience applause, video questions and intrusive tweets, politicians are seen sitting next to comedians, actors, novelists, journalists, former political advisers, musicians and the ubiquitous "social commentator." On this playing field, every opinion appears equal. A politician's statement regarding government policies seems no more authoritative than any other panel member's. Politicians jockey for space with a motley crew of entertainers and activists, all of who have their own barrows to push. Journalists, now celebrities in their own right, offer their "interpretations" of the political zeitgeist with impassioned pleas to camera. At times, it is difficult to tell the journalist from the politician, the comedian from the commentator. They all have "an opinion." In this great democratic wash, any authority and respect politicians once carried by virtue of their position has long since evaporated. We expect politicians to both govern and entertain us. And our assessment of their electability is all too often based on a hasty, shallow judgment of their ability to perform for the camera.

While Tingle did mention the destructive effects of the 24/7 media culture on our political debate, she could have perhaps spent more time revealing just how destructive the constant pressure for new angles, stories and analysis can be. In this new media climate, particularly in the political context of a struggling minority government, journalists increasingly tend to compete in an effort to draw bold, dramatic, black-and-white conclusions that will actually shape the course of politics itself. As the media watch every breath and analyse every utterance politicians make (a process that leeches politics of all spontaneity and exhausts the audience through the deluge of commentary it produces), political realities are created and smashed in a nanosecond. Clinging to the latest poll results, journalists who at the beginning of the week called for leadership speculation to stop can be found demanding the prime minister's resignation by the week's end. Journalists who pour scorn on politicians for their inconsistency and poor judgment might do well to look back over their past columns and see just how changeable their own political proclamations have been. All of the political class bear some responsibility for the quality of our political debate.

Whatever the reasons might be for the national anger Tingle has diagnosed, they are manifold and often hard to pin down. In addition to her own conclusions and those I've mentioned above, we could also add the increasingly pernicious influence of a poll-driven political culture, the tired predictability of the adversarial parliamentary system and the failure of the electorate itself to face up to its own shortcomings. Rather than wallow in the culture of complaint, blaming governments for every ill in our lives, we might take more responsibility for our actions, particularly our financial decisions, and the culture of massive individual debt that our obsession with home ownership and property speculation has created. And while the electorate rightly craves stable, honest and visionary political leadership, our politicians deserve to be accorded more respect and understanding than we seem willing to give them.

Mark McKenna

Greg Jericho

Laura Tingle ends her essay *Great Expectations* by arguing that we need a captain like Magellan to help the nation traverse the angry waters ahead. Given that Magellan died in the Philippines at around the halfway mark of his ship's circumnavigation of the globe, this does not bode well for whoever deems him or herself brave enough to take charge of the good ship Australia.

Tingle's essay seeks to paint Australia as an angry nation since our earliest times, but argues that the particular sense of anger pervading our recent political debates is linked to the fundamental shifts in economic policies that occurred from the 1980s under Hawke and Keating, which took the country from a closed and rather controlled economy to one where we became a cork floating on the international economic oceans.

The anger towards economic changes, however, is rather different from previous anger that has occurred in our history. I well recall in my university days in the early 1990s taking to the streets to march with supposed fury at the decision by the Hawke government to introduce HECS – shouting, "Education for all, not just the rich!" But even at the time my friends and I had little anger in us, because we realised that marching to protest having to pay for our own education was not quite the same as taking to the streets to protest the Vietnam War.

Similarly last year when the Occupy movement came to Australia, after an initial flush that provided solid numbers for a rally on its first weekend, the movement petered out and, despite an over-the-top reaction by the Victorian government, there was little evidence of widespread anger in the community regarding the changing economic nature of the country.

The anger that I see in evidence does not stir from the public at large, but mostly from an element of our society Tingle largely ignores: the media. She is right to point out that Kevin Rudd attempted to change the narrative concerning the role of government, but his great failure was to do this while keeping the words of the Howard government. When Tingle notes that one could almost hear a "sharp intake of breath among journalists in the press gallery as the treasurer was asked … whether the times might actually call for going into (gulp) deficit," she reveals that the press gallery, too, remained hostage to the narrative of the Howard government. Wayne Swan and Kevin Rudd went to such comical lengths to avoid mentioning the "D word" of deficit that it is perhaps not unsurprising that the media have continued to regard a surplus as conclusive evidence of good economic management. It is, however, inconclusive that this failure fully to adopt a new economic narrative led to any anger among the public.

There was more than enough confected anger from various media organisations regarding the stimulus package, where a metonymic approach saw any negative part reported as evidence of the whole lacking worth. Were one to read some of the newspapers, one would assume that every school in the country has a poorly built, overpriced hall. Obviously bad news sells, but you would hope the broader picture is also worth something.

But it was after the election that we saw the full anger of the media revealed, and the predictions of Crikey blogger Possum Comitatus of a state of (as he called it) "unhinging" come to be realised. Once the government pressed forward with a price on carbon, Sydney radio stations and newspapers were only too eager to fan any flames that were around. The Daily Telegraph, in a sequel to its attempts to bring about an early NSW state election, led the calls for a plebiscite on the policy, suggesting that for the government to introduce a price on carbon was "profoundly undemocratic." While attending one of the anti-carbon tax rallies promoted by Sydney radio, I saw a great deal of anger – anger stoked by the statements of those such as Alan Jones who would wish to see Julia Gillard and Bob Brown drowned in a chaff bag – statements that provide a lead to banners seen at the rally such as "Ditch the Witch." It was an anger that members of the Opposition – including Tony Abbott – were only too eager to embrace.

Tingle notes that after this year's budget the Australian reported on a family feeling aggrieved despite having an income of more than $258,000. Such a report is not "news" in the sense of reporting a public statement; nor is it really evidence that a broad section of the community thinks it should get something for nothing. What the report does reveal, however, is that the Australian believes such views are worth seeking out and reporting – a rather surprising tack from a paper that apparently favours prudent government spending. Tingle writes that, "This battler was oblivious to the idea that the rebate might have been just another form of welfare." Clearly, when we have reached a stage where newspapers will seek out people earning over $250,000 and treat them as "battlers," it is little wonder that such obliviousness exists. Were the battler to read most of the newspapers or listen to talkback radio in this country, she would remain oblivious – indeed, she would have her perception reinforced.

There may be anger in the community about the carbon tax, but it does not come from nowhere – nor does it come purely from our history of mistrusting politicians. The big change in the past three years is that we now have an activist media, one that seeks to make news as much as report it, one that seeks to control and determine elections – whether it be through forcing the leaders to attend "people's forums," criticising a particular policy, or going further and suggesting that the current government is undemocratic or illegitimate.

If this country is to find a Magellan prepared to brave the angry seas, he or she must realise that the media now takes a greater delight than ever before in a rough voyage and is doing all it can to blow off-course political parties that it does not favour. Rather than calling forth a brave captain ready to chart a dangerous passage, the situation leads me to suspect that future leaders may instead choose to paddle safely in the political shallows.

Greg Jericho

Percy Allan

Laura Tingle's sweeping history of Australia convincingly demonstrates that we have had a strong expectation of government entitlement and paternalism since being a penal colony. However, I suspect we share that trait with other Western democracies bar the United States, which exhibits suspicion and antipathy to the state because it was originally settled by refugees fleeing religious and political persecution in Europe.

When the average age of the workforce was low and there were many workers for each dependent child and retiree, politicians introduced generous health, aged-care and pension entitlements without the fiscal impact being felt immediately. But as the population aged, there were fewer workers per dependant to fund the welfare state through taxes, fees and charges. Governments then turned to debt, since that deferred the cost of current services to future generations. But the global financial crisis of 2007–09 required governments of the developed world to rescue banks and insurance companies by socialising their bad debts. Governments also ran up large budget deficits to fill the spending void left by households and investors. Central banks printed the money to buy bank and government securities that could not be sold to private investors.

We have now reached a point where both governments and central banks have exhausted their ammunition. The social democratic agenda has reached its taxation and debt limits just as the baby-boom generation moves into retirement, putting further cost pressures on the state. Having been dunked by the GFC, government is about to be drowned by past promises of entitlements whose costs will soar. Instead of having one dependant supported through the tax system by many workers, the future is Florida, where for every dependant there will be only one worker.

This will require a rationalisation of the role of the state, and with it government programs and personal entitlements. Norman Lindsay's magic pudding, where the more you cut the more you got, will turn into a shrinking pie, where the beneficiaries bicker and fight over what should be their fair share. The basic premise on which Western democracy was built after World War II, namely that the state could offer more than people paid in tax, has been exhausted. From here on, the challenge for politicians will be how to cut government provisions without hurting the most vulnerable. This will require them to persuade the self-sufficient majority to support the disadvantaged and marginalised minority. Whether politicians accustomed to appealing to the hip-pocket nerve can summon up the leadership qualities to sell hard times to a cynical electorate will be the acid test of whether modern democracy survives.

Upper- and middle-class welfare will have to be withdrawn so that only the genuinely needy are subsidised. Mutual obligation will supplement means-testing to ensure that all able-bodied persons of working age receive social security or other forms of welfare only as a temporary measure to help them return to the workforce. The concept of the "deserving poor," so loathed by welfare agencies, will return to centre-stage. Green taxes will be one of the few ways for governments to justify raising new revenue, since private capital as well as professional labour will be sufficiently mobile to avoid high-taxing jurisdictions. Consumption tax payments will slump as households save more to repay the massive debts they ran up during the credit binge from 1995 to 2007.

Indeed the private and public debt overhang is causing asset deflation and subdued growth which is generating heightened political conflict. Yet Australia is one of the few places where banks and governments have relatively strong balance sheets. We missed the worst of the 2000 dotcom bust because we had few technology companies. We enjoyed a commodity boom thanks largely to China's voracious appetite for our natural resources. Unlike in other Western countries our commercial banks survived the 2008 global financial meltdown thanks to government regulations that prohibited them from over-gearing. Also, the Commonwealth government came to the rescue of the banks by guaranteeing their deposits and foreign loans, handing out cash to the public and going on a spending spree. It worked, but as Laura Tingle observes, few voters appreciated its economic purpose, seeing it instead as a return to Whitlam-era profligacy.

The relevance of the share market to politics should not be underestimated. Recent research shows that the best predictor of American presidential races has not been the rate of unemployment, but the state of the stock market. If it was bullish the incumbent party won, and if it was bearish it lost.

Since 2000, most of the developed world has been in a "secular bear market," a technical term meaning that share prices have at best swung sideways (Europe and America) or at worst swung downwards (Japan). Research also shows that secular bear markets are marked by an increase in social and political discord and conflict. Tribalism, whether based on race, creed, nationality or culture, intensifies during hard times. As society fractures, solidarity grows within each disparate group, while outsiders are viewed with growing antipathy.

The secular bear markets since the end of the nineteenth century have been 1901–21, 1929–49, 1966–82 and 2000–? These periods have been marked by national unrest and international conflict – World War I, World War II and the start of the Cold War, the Vietnam War and more recently the War on Terror, Iraq and Afghanistan.

Secular bear markets are marked by dark social moods where nations turn inward, become xenophobic and look for simple and direct answers from their politicians. Such episodes throw up both demagogues (such as Lenin, Hitler and, locally, Jack Lang who, while no monster, basked in his followers' slogan, "Lang is Greater than Lenin") and statesmen (Winston Churchill, Franklin Roosevelt and, locally, John Curtin). They contrast with the outward, engaging, hopeful and trusting spirit that reigns during secular bull markets.

The relevance of this to Australia? Since Australia joined the global secular bear market in late 2007, its mood, like that of the rest of the developed world, has become despondent. Respected economic columnists, such as Ross Gittins and Jessica Irvine, argue that Australians have no reason to be gloomy and cranky because they have never had it so good. After all, Australia was spared the GFC and has enjoyed the benefits of low unemployment, real wages growth, cheaper imports and overseas holidays thanks to the mining boom.

But notwithstanding glowing economic results, Australians remain deeply worried. We missed the bullet of the GFC by a hair's breadth and we know it. True, our banks remained strong because our home prices held up instead of plunging as they did in America. That was because Australia has a housing shortage rather than a glut. But several global surveys show we have among the highest residential property prices in the world. Also, our households have the highest mortgage debt to disposable income ratio recorded anywhere in the world – even higher than in America, where excessive housing debt precipitated the GFC.

Unlike America's, our housing bubble so far has adjusted through rents escalating rather than price sharply plummeting. However, new families now find themselves not only unable to afford to buy a house, but also unable to rent one.

As for those in or approaching retirement, their superannuation savings are depressed because the Australian share market has drifted down after recovering half the value of its 2009 fall. While general inflation has remained modest, huge rises in electricity prices have retirees worried that their bills will outrun their nest eggs. Meanwhile the profile of the labour market is changing from full-time permanent work to part-time temporary work. Newly arrived immigrants (especially from Asia and other underdeveloped countries) are not reluctant to accept such jobs, but Australians trained for a career or trade find such work below their expectations.

The commodity boom that has kept Australia out of harm's way has by all accounts peaked. Whether it will be followed by a commodity crash is too early to say, but mining and energy companies have foreshadowed a slowdown in investment plans and even the scrapping of some projects already in the pipeline. The rest of the economy for the last decade has not been achieving the productivity gains to bolster our living standards should the mining sector go off the boil.

If our terms of trade deteriorate further, we could get an economic shock that would undermine our housing market through higher unemployment and interest rates (as foreign capital would become more expensive to access). Business cost-cutting would accelerate. This is what scares a lot of Australians, who know their high mortgages are only affordable while they have a job and interest rates remain low.

Of course, Australia's low government debt and relatively high interest rates mean that we have a fiscal and monetary arsenal sufficient to counter any international shock, at least initially. But Australians suspect our luck won't last indefinitely – we simply don't have the faith in China's political stability and uninterrupted growth that our policy-makers have. We worry that at any moment we could be caught up in the international financial crisis, which our personal debt loads leave us ill-equipped to handle without massive government assistance.

So much of Australia's present sense of entitlement has to do with wanting assurance that if the worst happens, the government has a contingency plan to rescue families heavily indebted from the credit binge of the 1990s and 2000s. A premium is now being placed on certainty, security and stability – economically, politically, socially and regionally.

Having a minority government facing a truculent opposition is unsettling to most voters given the economic and political troubles in Europe and America, two blocs that previously ensured world order. Being torn between the American alliance for military security and Chinese trade pacts for economic security adds to our sense of anxiety.

Furthermore, the negative mood associated with the global secular bear market is poisoning local politics – making it more adversarial and venomous. Times like these are not conducive to bipartisan trust and cooperation, but they do make voters more receptive to big thinking and new ideas. Crises always generate reflection and change.

Should Australia continue to escape the contagion threatening insolvent sovereign states and financial institutions abroad, it may well join the upbeat mood of our near neighbours to the north. How well we integrate with Asia as economic and political power shifts from west to east will determine our destiny for much of this century.

Australians are very scared of losing our traditional lifestyles and entitlements. It's time politicians told us the stark truth that to cope with an ageing population and a faltering commodities boom, government will need to be there for those in genuine need, but the rest of us will have to pay our own way.

In future being Australian won't guarantee a higher living standard than being Asian. Instead educational attainment will determine personal income regardless of race or nationality, with governments forced to apply their scarce resources to only the most pressing causes. The public bureaucracy will eventually confine itself to what it does best – steering, not rowing. In other words, to making and funding public policy while leaving service delivery to the most reliable and affordable providers chosen either by government tender or citizen voucher. The myth that public services and transfer payments are costless will be shattered as politicians are forced to make hard choices between competing needs and alternative suppliers. Australians are in for a rude awakening, though hopefully one less severe and prolonged than in the rest of the developed world.

Of course, an alternative scenario is that governments decide to buy their way out of trouble by printing money to meet their existing obligations and forgive private debt. That might work for as long as a country's currency is accepted as international tender, but the history of South America suggests it invites military coup d'états or the election of autocrats to restore civil order and monetary stability. Australia is not Argentina, but the great democracies of the world will be sorely tested as they undergo the Great Deleveraging – just as they were during the Great Depression.

Percy Allan

Michael Keating

Australians have always expected government to act as a "utility" providing for
their welfare, as the historian Keith Hancock remarked in his history of Australia
published back in 1930. In important respects the problem of these expectations
running ahead of capacity is not exactly new. Nor is it a problem that is unique
to Australia. This incompatibility of expectations and capacity was arguably a
critical cause of the stagflation of the 1970s and into the 1980s.

Stagflation emerged initially in the United States when Lyndon Johnson raised
expectations through the introduction of his "Great Society," but the American
people and their Congress then refused to cover the cost of both the expansion
of government and the Vietnam War. Similarly in Australia, stagflation became
a much more severe problem after the Whitlam government responded to rising
public expectations about new and increased services, but again lacked the
means to pay for them. Whitlam's own expectation was that the additional cost
would be covered through economic growth, but rising inflation of itself led to
lower economic growth. Eventually Australia did manage to deal with stagflation, but like other countries, not without some pain. Unemployment rose as a
result of the structural adjustments involved in making the economy more competitive and less inflation-prone, and also because the "recession we had to have"
was critical to reducing inflationary expectations.

The point is that the incompatibility of expectations and government capacity
has quite a long history. Resolving such a problem will most likely have difficult
political consequences, so it is not surprising that governments may seek to
spend years trying to "muddle through," often with a certain degree of success.
In that case, Australia appears to be in relatively good shape compared to the
United States and other advanced nations in Europe. In those countries the mis-
match between expectations and capacity has led to mountains of debt, and
much more difficult decisions will be required.

Much of Laura Tingle's essay is built on the assertion that government capacity has been reduced, as "politicians no longer control interest rates, the exchange rate, or wages [and] prices." But that raises the questions of whether governments ever did control these key prices, why the changes were made, and how effective the new arrangements are.

First, governments have never controlled *real* interest rates or the *real* exchange rate, and these real, not nominal, rates have always been the critical variables affecting economic activity. Furthermore, Australia, except during the national emergency of World War II, has never had government control of even nominal prices and wages, let alone their *real* equivalents.

Second, countries that have a fixed exchange rate find that they do have to change their rate from time to time, as it falls out of line with their competitors' rates or in response to capital flows. Such pressures have, of course, grown as a consequence of globalisation, but they did not start with globalisation.

Third, any attempt to fix the nominal exchange rate against another country's currency, such as the US dollar, means that the ability to conduct an independent monetary policy is thereby surrendered. Instead, the country is then forced to adopt monetary policy settings consistent with the US position, with interest rates set to follow those in the United States so as to ensure that the exchange rate does not move.

In short, far from deregulating financial markets because all such regulation was "bad," as Tingle asserts, our government under Hawke and Keating changed the nature of financial regulation to make it more effective in a globalised world economy. For the first time, we gained the capacity to run a monetary policy independent of other countries, and the benefits of this can be seen in how we have managed largely to avoid each of the major recessions in partner countries since 1991. Surely that is an improvement in government control and capacity.

Tingle's concerns about the quality of public services and our willingness to pay are nearer the mark. Indeed, as she suggests, this is a subject worthy of more public debate. But again it would help if we keep the following facts in mind.

We are overall a very lightly taxed nation compared to other advanced countries that aspire to similar standards of health, education and welfare. And we have also managed to provide these services without incurring excessive debt.

Taxation has more or less stayed around its present level since the mid-1970s. Tax reform over the last forty years has been about changing the structure of taxation – who pays – and not about the overall level of revenue collected.

A number of respected commentators have raised concerns about the future fiscal outlook, partly because of the consequences of an ageing population, and partly in response to the demands for new and higher quality services, such as for the disabled and for children. But before we conclude that future service provision will require higher taxation we need to consider the consequences for and of economic growth.

On the one hand, many of the arguments that various lower taxes will lead to higher economic growth are not supported by any evidence. Indeed, judging from recent experience, higher taxation of superannuation would very likely lead to greater saving.

On the other hand, as Skills Australia and the Productivity Commission have separately shown, increased investment in education and training, directed particularly to improving the employability skills of those on the margin of the labour force, would increase the rate of employment participation from the present rate of 65 per cent to 69 per cent by around 2025. This would in turn result in sufficient extra economic output and taxation revenue to meet the demands for the additional government expenditure projected over that period by the Treasury Intergenerational Report without an increase in taxation.

These facts do not suggest that the Age of Entitlement is necessarily unaffordable and over, as Tingle approvingly quotes Joe Hockey as concluding. Indeed, that might not necessarily be true anywhere. The so-called debt-laden countries in Europe are not those countries most associated with the welfare state, such as Scandinavia, Germany and Holland, none of which is experiencing any great difficulties.

Finally, a word on the changing nature of government services. Before the mid-nineteenth century, services such as health and education were largely delivered by non-government providers. When government took over these services, it was influenced by a desire for greater uniformity of provision. At the time this was justified on equity grounds, where equity was defined as similar treatment of all. Today, by contrast, we are a much more individualistic society, and equity is often, although not always, conceived of as equality of opportunity or sometimes even as equality of outcomes. But equality of opportunity or outcomes requires an approach that focuses much more on the particular needs of each individual instead of aiming for uniform provision.

The comparative advantage of the state was, however, in uniform provision. Thus the shift in focus to meeting individual needs has required a variety of providers, with individuals able to exercise their choice. But especially where the state pays for the service it still retains overall and effective control over what is effectively a "managed market." The state determines the number of places and who accesses them and on what terms. The state also specifies through its contract arrangements the quality of service provision. Often the contract speci-fications are not materially different from the instructions that it once provided to its own employees. If there is a difference, it is in giving more recognition to professional discretion and extending the opportunity for consumer choice.

Michael Keating

Andrew Leigh

In 2002, David Moss described the role of government as being the ultimate "risk manager." Governments, Moss believed, ought to act as a backstop for things that might go wrong in our lives. Just as we buy private insurance to pool our risk with other customers, so governments allow us to pool social risk across other citizens. You can think of your taxes partly as an insurance premium.

The notion of government as risk manager doesn't cover the full gamut of what governments do, but it does encapsulate many of their important roles. For example, governments help guard against overseas threats and keep our streets safe. Managing risk explains why we have a social safety net to guard against the risk of poverty, a public health care system to deal with the risk of illness, and a public education system to remove the risk that poor parents might not be able to afford to educate their children.

In the personal tax system, progressive taxation reflects the fact that those of us who earn above-average incomes tend to have been fortunate in our family background, educational opportunities and career breaks. The company tax system considers risk in the way it allows a firm to carry forward losses from bad years to offset profits in good years. The rubric of risk also reminds us that governmental responses to floods and bushfires need to be compassionate, yet not perversely encourage people to build homes in even riskier places.

Risk isn't the only framework through which to view policy. For example, my colleague Bill Shorten prefers to describe government as consisting of four pillars: the minimum wage, the age pension, compulsory superannuation and Medicare, to which we have now added a National Disability Insurance Scheme. But as an economist, I'd prefer to view the NDIS as a form of risk management. Each of us is just a car crash away from a profound disability, a dice roll in the genetic lottery from giving birth to a child with a congenital abnormality.

If government is the ultimate risk manager, then society needs to decide which risks should be borne by citizens, and which should be taken on by governments. There's no right answer to this, but it's easy to see differences across countries. Many of the risks that are borne by individuals in the United States are carried by the government in Sweden. In some contexts, governments should be encouraging risk-taking (we want our scientists and entrepreneurs to take a chance). In other situations, we need to ensure that we don't privatise the gains and socialise the losses, as Wall Street seems to have done over recent decades.

How a government manages risk says a lot about its values. Reading Laura Tingle's analysis of Howard-era social policy, I was struck by how daily politics utterly dominated good policy. In place of risk management, we got – in Tingle's memorable phrase – "endless avuncular tax cuts and new cash entitlements." I am yet to meet anyone who can persuade me that the proper role for government includes providing the baby bonus to a millionaire.

All this came at a cost. As John Howard expanded non-means-tested benefits, he once said: "People like getting a cheque from the government." What he failed to mention was something known as the deadweight cost of taxation. For every $100 raised in revenue, around $20 is lost in decreased work effort and entrepreneurial activity. Churning money for its own sake means that there's less to go around. As George Megalogenis noted recently, "The competition for handouts affected the [Howard] government itself." On social policy, Howard seemed incapable of lowering expectations when the times called for it.

Tingle is right to focus on the difficult politics of who gets what in Australia. Her story of the Adelaide family that earns over $258,000 and rails against the government for means-testing the private health insurance rebate reminds me of several constituents who wrote to make the same point. And yet our government is not the first to have made hard decisions on means-testing. When the Hawke government put an assets test on the pension in the mid-1980s, the Opposition leader, Andrew Peacock, called it "the latest of this Government's assaults on the elderly," and promised to repeal it if the Coalition won office. Today, the pension assets test is an accepted part of our social policy.

What I find a bit harder to cop is Joe Hockey lecturing from London about the need for the "Age of Entitlement" to cease. When Labor froze indexation on a family tax benefit supplement and scaled back the outdated dependent spouse tax offset, Hockey fulminated in parliament: "Your budget is indifferent to the plight of your people." On Sky TV, he said, "I think this is madness." To the *Australian* newspaper, he said, "I despise this envy; this envy and this jealousy." His former leader Malcolm Turnbull used similar language when we means-tested the baby bonus to families earning under $150,000 (excluding the richest 6 per cent of parents). Hockey's London speech raises some interesting questions, but when you put it together with his views about means-testing, it's hard to avoid the conclusion that Hockey wants the Age of Entitlement to end for the poor, but continue for the rich.

The former New York governor Mario Cuomo once said that politicians campaign in poetry, but govern in prose. A corollary is that while politicians campaign in "and," we govern in "or." Each decision to spend in one area makes it harder to devote resources to another area. And every government decision to spend requires that money be raised from taxes on land, labour or capital. As Milton Friedman famously put it, "to tax is to spend." These trade-offs – these "or" questions – mean that a government with a thousand priorities might as well have no priorities at all. Tingle might have usefully pointed out that on this score, the Gillard government has been more willing to make trade-offs than our predecessors. For example, Stephen Koukoulas recently observed that during their combined total of more than twenty years in office, the Fraser and Howard governments never once cut their real spending. By contrast, Labor governments have cut real spending on five occasions since the mid-1980s.

Tingle writes fondly about the Hawke–Keating reform era, in which, "The political debate was not taking place at the level of what the reforms might mean for the individual, or what citizens could expect of governments in the future; it was being fought at the level of institutions, such as the centralised wage-fixing system, and the national economy." This is a good principle for reform, particularly as a counterpoint to the "everyone's a winner" reform mantra of the Howard government. Reforms without losers are rare, but that doesn't mean governments should eschew all reform.

This dynamic is particularly complicated when one realises that politicians are often forced to carry out reforms during an economic crisis. At this point, leaders can more credibly say, "The system is broken; we cannot go on like this." And yet from an economic standpoint, it is far preferable to carry out reforms in boom times, since there are more resources available to compensate those who are made worse off. In the mid-1980s, the strong economy allowed tariff cuts to be accompanied by a steel plan; a car plan; a textile, clothing and footwear plan; a shipbuilding plan; and a heavy engineering adjustment and development program. And yet there were many who looked at the strength of the macro-economy and wondered why we needed to reduce industry protection at all.

Perhaps I've spent too long walking on the sunny side of the street, but I think the "angry Australian" Tingle describes is a passing mood rather than a national trait. Yet that doesn't take much away from her astute analysis of the challenge of reform. Governments will always be able to think of more good ways to spend government dollars than the Treasury coffers permit. So rationing our spending – and clearly explaining the reasons for our choices – is a challenge that will always be with us. It will probably also place more challenges on parliamentarians like me to define the boundaries of a good government. For that, the notion of government as risk manager may not be a bad spot to start.

Andrew Leigh

John Burnheim

One reason why people like strong leaders is that they know it is often better for coherent decisions to be made and implemented than matters to drift in a sea of pointless wheeling and dealing. A Keating or a Howard may be taking us in wrong directions, but at least we think they know what they are doing. We think we know what they are up to. They succeed in convincing most of us that they are not just manipulators, much less scarcely hanging on to power or serving some narrow interests, but are fundamentally concerned about what sort of society we shall live in. Sometimes they may be forced into "political" decisions, but usually they seem to be able to rise above such dubious compromises, judging by what they see as the national interests.

It is increasingly difficult to be such a leader, for many reasons relating to social changes, communications and the demise of old mythologies, but above all because the elements that make up the national interests have become immensely complex and differentiated. We have multiplied our needs and raised our aspirations in every aspect of our lives, including all the services that governments have been required to supply, from the traditional areas of public works and regulation of private and public conduct to the modern concerns of economics, education, health and welfare. Ultimately the conflicting demands on our resources are resolved in the national budget as a complex compromise between various forms of taxation and items of expenditure. The budget evolves out of the structure of existing entitlements and bureaucratic practices. The fundamental principle of bureaucracy is working to rules laid down from above. In a democracy that means treating everybody by the same criteria, and in practice it means providing them with the same product in the interests of efficiency and cheapness.

In societies emerging from poverty, public provision of many services means that people come to enjoy services they have not been brought up to expect.

People can be proud of the institutions that provide those goods. Even very limited services are not only a bonus to the individual, but a focus of a shared identity. In aspirational consumer societies, by contrast, the standard provision almost inevitably appears to the consumer as an inadequate ration, especially when compared with what appear as lavish provisions in matters outside their concerns. Everybody feels that their concerns are entitled to greater consideration and often that they are bearing an unfair share of the burden of public expenditure. The state apparatus becomes the focus of conflict, complaint and disaffection.

In this consumerist context, political involvement of citizens languishes. In any case it is increasingly pointless, given the professionalisation of politics. Agitation by special-interest groups replaces attempts to change policy through involvement in the party. Even protest is professionalised. Voting is like buying in the market. If Labor doesn't supply what you want, you vote for somebody else. On the other hand, the professional politicians rely increasingly on the techniques of advertising to package their services in a way that will look attractive to swinging voters, to respond to the most vociferous and fashionable lobbies, following rather than leading, trying to be "with it." That in turn leads to disillusionment. We want serious, well-thought-out policies.

Many people have concluded that it is important to disentangle crucial issues from the power trading and have them deliberated publicly by the sort of people who are going to bear the consequences of whatever decision is adopted. The assumption is that if citizens representative of the constituencies most affected by an issue are brought together, given the assistance of relevant experts and time to deliberate in an attempt to find the best solution to a problem, they are more likely to arrive at a decision that is more sensitive and constructive than that of either the experts or the politicians, who are more remote from the concerns of ordinary people and more addicted to standard prescriptions. Starting with academic suggestions, such involvement has attracted even conservative politicians. New Democracy, a local foundation devoted to promoting these ideas, has attracted the active support of former premiers Nick Greiner and Geoff Gallup, for example.

Among the aims of such bodies is building up in the community a lot more trust in decisions and a much better understanding of the possibilities of finding common ground once simplistic presuppositions and irrelevant deals are abandoned. These "citizen juries" or elements of deliberative democracy have been tried in many countries throughout the world, but on an episodic scale. It has been shown repeatedly that in the course of involvement in such deliberations people do change their opinions, and that the result is commonly a high degree of satisfaction among the participants. Unfortunately, the movement has nowhere near reached the scale where its benefits can be understood by the general public and the authority of such bodies accepted.

When Julia Gillard proposed such a body to come up with a response to climate change, she was ridiculed almost universally, even by Laura Tingle. It was seen as just another political ploy. When Nick Greiner, having been put in charge of transport planning in New South Wales, proposed a citizen body to determine its priorities, he was told, "That's what we're paying you to do!" The consumerist assumption is that you ought to be able to buy good government off the shelf. Of course, politicians make much of "consultation with the people." But the crucial difference is that when consulted, people will tell you what they would like or which presentation looks more attractive. They are not being asked to look at a problem and count the costs of dealing with it effectively. They are not being educated. Nor are the politicians.

You can only vote for what is on offer. At present in all levels of government we have to accept one or other of very big packages, much of which we do not want, put together by a defective process of decision. We compensate to some extent by agitating against the winners on specific points. Until we evolve a better decision-making process, the prospects for a healthy political climate are very dim. You cannot have democracy without an appreciation of what makes for good decisions.

John Burnheim

Laura Tingle

When Tony Abbott returned from his trip to Washington and Beijing in late July, he checked in with his interviewer of choice, Alan Jones. The broadcaster sought to get Abbott to agree with him on a range of issues, including asylum seekers, the Greens, foreign investment, and even a rather unusual digression suggesting we should get rid of Medicare.

But towards the end of the interview, Jones – who was broadcasting from the Olympic Games in London – got to "the reason I actually wanted to speak to you."

"When people talk about the failure of the Rudd and Gillard governments," Jones fulminated, "they talk about FuelWatch and GroceryWatch and Pink Batts and Building the Education Revolution and the National Broadband Network and carbon taxes and mining taxes.

"I mean, it goes on and on. No one ever talks about sport."

Yes, that's right. Alan Jones went on to blame Julia Gillard for the fact that Australia, a couple of days into the Games, wasn't winning many medals.

This was a bridge too far even for Abbott who, when he eventually got a word in, diplomatically said he was "inclined to look at what happens in these Olympics before I rush to conclusions about whether our existing programs are adequate or not."

A week earlier, Leigh Sales had interviewed the prime minister on the ABC's 7.30. "The inflation figure that was out today was low," Sales observed, "but when we look over the past few years at the cost of the goods and services that Australians cannot live without – things like electricity and gas and water – they have risen enormously. Why hasn't Labor eased cost-of-living pressures on Australians since it's come to office, as it promised to do?"

These two interviews go to the heart of the point I was trying to make in my Quarterly Essay. That is because they betray the explicit, or implicit, expectations that shape our modern-day politics: expectations that are reflected in, and amplified by, the media. For some of these expectations, politicians have no one but themselves to blame. For others, the media must take some responsibility, as reporters and commentators have become more and more prone to placing expectations on politicians that they can't possibly meet.

The "cost of living" is an example of an issue about which we are always being told that people feel angry. But it is also an issue that people feel they have a right to be angry about because the Labor government said it was going to do something about easing the impact of rising prices.

Where it once was used to refer to a high inflation rate, the cost of living is now a term of political abuse. Federal Labor heard the angst about cost-of-living pressures from focus groups before the 2007 election – when it meant things like soaring petrol prices and falling housing affordability – and sensed an opportunity. It promised programs to target petrol and grocery prices. The federal Coalition has subsequently taken up the phrase and applied it to spiralling energy and water charges.

Whether Australians win lots of gold medals at the Olympics is a result of a range of factors, only one of which is sports funding by governments, and in particular, sports funding by any particular government. Had people been arguing before the Olympics in London that there wasn't enough funding going into elite sport?

Some of my correspondents take me to task for not discussing the role of the media in our modern anger. The role of the media was also the subject of many questions at forums in Sydney and Melbourne about the essay.

Mark McKenna, for example, suggests I am "understandably reticent to place [my] own profession under the same harsh light of examination that [I apply] to politicians."

Actually, I have written a number of pieces about the media's role in the current madness (for example, "Falling Down the Miners' Shaft," July 2010, and "Shut Down in Sideshow Alley," July 2011, both in the *Walkley Magazine* and available online). Others have written copiously on the subject. I did not address it in this essay, partly because I had been there before, and more importantly because I wanted to consider, and provoke others to consider, the underlying premise of the anger that the media sometimes feed.

For it seems to me that in the tussle we have seen between the media and government in recent years, the fault lies in both the questions and the answers.

The media has slipped too easily into asking, "What is the government going to do about it?" rather than first asking, "*Should* the government do something about it?" or, indeed, "*Can* the government do something about it?"

For their part, politicians have also become too reluctant to say, "Well, the government can't or shouldn't do something about it," and too prepared to suggest they can fix things when they can't.

Somewhere in this process, somebody should be stopping to ask whether there are just some things that can't be reduced to the simple presumption that if there is a problem, it has to be fixed by government.

Sure, sections of the media have led, or misled, the public into holding all sorts of warped views of political events in the past five years. It appals me as much as anybody else. But I believe the greatest disservice of the media has been not just to distort facts or exaggerate them. It has been to imply that government is all-powerful if it chooses to be, that there is an exact science to the way you run policy and politics, and that, therefore, any slip-up along the way is abnormal, even catastrophic.

The cost of living is not something that can always be addressed by government policy – as Labor found to its detriment long before the carbon tax came along. It suggested that it could do something about petrol prices, for example, when the world oil market and the complexities of retailing petrol made this virtually impossible.

Equally, the cost of living may rise as a direct result of government policies, such as electricity-market deregulation or privatisation. The question then becomes whether it makes sense for the government to offer to compensate people for increases in the cost of living when its own policies – designed to send better price signals to the market – are responsible.

Having argued in 2007 that it could do something about the cost of living, Labor got stuck with its own rhetoric. Having opened the cost-of-living can of worms, it has been timid about closing it again. It has cruelled its capacity to boast about an almost unique international economic performance because it has become so entrapped by the need to make constant acknowledgment that people are suffering because of cost-of-living pressures.

Is it, therefore, unreasonable of Leigh Sales to ask the prime minister why the government hasn't met its promise to ease such pressures, since Labor said it would do so? No.

But, political promises aside, is it reasonable to expect that the federal government should compensate households for the fact that power bills are rising as a result of both state government and private sector decisions? No.

Nonetheless, the expectation has become entrenched that this is what the federal government should do, and neither the media nor politicians stop and say, "Wait a minute! Since when did governments have to compensate people for price rises? Particularly price rises imposed by other levels of government?"

There is fault on both sides here, because politicians make promises to ease pressures and because the media insist that these promises be met when it is not at all clear that, on rational policy grounds, they should be met. The result is more fodder for a media cycle that has too often reduced politics to an ongoing soap opera rather than a discussion of difficult issues that require balance-of-argument decisions.

Other correspondents have engaged in the broader questions I raise in the essay about what will happen to the role of government in the future, and Michael Keating has raised the question of whether politicians really controlled the things they claimed to control in the age before deregulation.

If you read the cabinet papers from this period, it brings home the delusion we all laboured under in those days. These papers contain bold predictions about where the economy was headed which, viewed from the safety of a period of floating exchange rates, we can see were even greater stabs in the dark than they might be these days.

In a world of fixed exchange rates we were, ironically, much more at the mercy of changing international fortunes than we are today. But control is in the eye of the beholder. And my point was that the political message of those times, and the bigger political compact after federation, rested on assertions to voters that politicians could indeed control key prices in the economy.

Some of the discussion that has followed the publication of the essay has been heartening. A focus on the notion of "entitlement" seems to have snuck into the political conversation.

Yet we are still confronted with a situation where both sides of politics career towards a 2013 election overloaded with pledges to implement policies that they cannot afford without a significant change in the way the federal government operates.

Laura Tingle

Percy Allan is a public policy, finance and management adviser and a former secretary of the NSW Treasury.

John Burnheim was an associate professor of philosophy at the University of Sydney and is the author of *Is Democracy Possible? The Alternative to Electoral Politics* (2006).

Greg Jericho is a political blogger, former public servant and author of *The Rise of the Fifth Estate: Social Media and Blogging in Australian Politics* (2012).

Michael Keating has been the head of the Australian public service and of various senior departments, including Prime Minister and Cabinet under the Hawke, Keating and Howard governments, and currently consults on economic policy. He is the author of *Who Rules? How Government Retains Control of a Privatised Economy* (2004).

Andrew Leigh is the federal member for Fraser, and a former professor of economics at the Australian National University. His most recent book is *Disconnected* (2010).

David Marr is the author of *Patrick White: A Life*, *The High Price of Heaven* and *Panic*, and co-author with Marian Wilkinson of *Dark Victory*. He has written for the *Sydney Morning Herald*, the *Age* and the *Monthly*, been editor of the *National Times*, a reporter for *Four Corners* and presenter of ABC TV's *Media Watch*. In 2010 he wrote the Walkley Award-winning Quarterly Essay *Power Trip: The Political Journey of Kevin Rudd*.

Mark McKenna is an associate professor of history at the University of Sydney. His latest book is *An Eye for Eternity: The Life of Manning Clark* (2011).

Laura Tingle is political editor of the *Australian Financial Review*. She won the Paul Lyneham Award for Excellence in Press Gallery Journalism in 2004, and Walkley awards in 2005 and 2011. In 2010 she was shortlisted for the John Button Prize for political writing. She appears regularly on Radio National's *Late Night Live* and ABC TV's *Insiders*.

John Wanna holds the Sir John Bunting Chair of Public Administration at the Australia and New Zealand School of Government, ANU.

SUBSCRIBE to Quarterly Essay & SAVE nearly 40% off the cover price

Subscriptions: Receive a discount and never miss an issue. Mailed direct to your door.
- ☐ **1 year subscription** (4 issues): $59 a year within Australia incl. GST. Outside Australia $89.
- ☐ **2 year subscription** (8 issues): $105 a year within Australia incl. GST. Outside Australia $165.
* All prices include postage and handling.

Back Issues: (Prices include postage and handling.)

- ☐ **QE 1** ($15.95) Robert Manne *In Denial*
- ☐ **QE 2** ($15.95) John Birmingham *Appeasing Jakarta*
- ☐ **QE 4** ($15.95) Don Watson *Rabbit Syndrome*
- ☐ **QE 6** ($15.95) John Button *Beyond Belief*
- ☐ **QE 7** ($15.95) John Martinkus *Paradise Betrayed*
- ☐ **QE 8** ($15.95) Amanda Lohrey *Groundswell*
- ☐ **QE 10** ($15.95) Gideon Haigh *Bad Company*
- ☐ **QE 11** ($15.95) Germaine Greer *Whitefella Jump Up*
- ☐ **QE 12** ($15.95) David Malouf *Made in England*
- ☐ **QE 13** ($15.95) Robert Manne with David Corlett *Sending Them Home*
- ☐ **QE 14** ($15.95) Paul McGeough *Mission Impossible*
- ☐ **QE 15** ($15.95) Margaret Simons *Latham's World*
- ☐ **QE 16** ($15.95) Raimond Gaita *Breach of Trust*
- ☐ **QE 17** ($15.95) John Hirst *"Kangaroo Court"*
- ☐ **QE 18** ($15.95) Gail Bell *The Worried Well*
- ☐ **QE 19** ($15.95) Judith Brett *Relaxed & Comfortable*
- ☐ **QE 20** ($15.95) John Birmingham *A Time for War*
- ☐ **QE 21** ($15.95) Clive Hamilton *What's Left?*
- ☐ **QE 22** ($15.95) Amanda Lohrey *Voting for Jesus*
- ☐ **QE 23** ($15.95) Inga Clendinnen *The History Question*

- ☐ **QE 24** ($15.95) Robyn Davidson *No Fixed Address*
- ☐ **QE 25** ($15.95) Peter Hartcher *Bipolar Nation*
- ☐ **QE 26** ($15.95) David Marr *His Master's Voice*
- ☐ **QE 27** ($15.95) Ian Lowe *Reaction Time*
- ☐ **QE 28** ($15.95) Judith Brett *Exit Right*
- ☐ **QE 29** ($15.95) Anne Manne *Love & Money*
- ☐ **QE 30** ($15.95) Paul Toohey *Last Drinks*
- ☐ **QE 31** ($15.95) Tim Flannery *Now or Never*
- ☐ **QE 32** ($15.95) Kate Jennings *American Revolution*
- ☐ **QE 33** ($15.95) Guy Pearse *Quarry Vision*
- ☐ **QE 34** ($15.95) Annabel Crabb *Stop at Nothing*
- ☐ **QE 36** ($15.95) Mungo MacCallum *Australian Story*
- ☐ **QE 37** ($15.95) Waleed Aly *What's Right?*
- ☐ **QE 38** ($15.95) David Marr *Power Trip*
- ☐ **QE 39** ($15.95) Hugh White *Power Shift*
- ☐ **QE 42** ($15.95) Judith Brett *Fair Share*
- ☐ **QE 43** ($15.95) Robert Manne *Bad News*
- ☐ **QE 44** ($15.95) Andrew Charlton *Man-Made World*
- ☐ **QE 45** ($15.95) Anna Krien *Us and Them*
- ☐ **QE 46** ($15.95) Laura Tingle *Great Expectations*

Payment Details: I enclose a cheque/money order made out to Schwartz Media Pty Ltd. Please debit my credit card (Mastercard or Visa accepted).

Card No. ☐☐☐☐ ☐☐☐☐ ☐☐☐☐ ☐☐☐☐

Expiry date /   **CCV**   **Amount $**

Cardholder's name   **Signature**

Name

Address

Email   **Phone**

Post or fax this form to: Quarterly Essay, Reply Paid 79448, Collingwood VIC 3066 / Tel: (03) 9486 0288 / Fax: (03) 9486 0244 / Email: subscribe@blackincbooks.com Subscribe online at **www.quarterlyessay.com**